Leadership for Transformation

Leadership for Transformation

Edited by
JoAnn Danelo Barbour
Gill Robinson Hickman

A Volume in the International Leadership Series
Building Leadership Bridges

International Leadership Association

JOSSEY-BASS
A Wiley Imprint
www.josseybass.com

Published by Jossey-Bass
A Wiley Imprint
989 Market Street, San Francisco, CA 94103-1741—www.josseybass.com

Jossey-Bass books and products are available through most bookstores. To contact Jossey-Bass directly call our Customer Care Department within the U.S. at 800-956-7739, outside the U.S. at 317-572-3986, or fax 317-572-4002.

Jossey-Bass also publishes its books in a variety of electronic formats. Some content that appears in print may not be available in electronic books.

ISBN 978-0-470-94668-8

Printed in the United States of America
FIRST EDITION
PB Printing   10 9 8 7 6 5 4 3 2 1

Contents

Transformation Through Artistry

Transformation in Practice

Leadership for Transformation

List of Contributors

JoAnn Danelo Barbour is professor of education administration and leadership at Texas Woman's University. Former chief editor of *Academic Exchange Quarterly*, her research interests are in multidisciplinary, artistic approaches to leading and teaching leadership. Recent publications include ten entries in the *Sage Encyclopedia of Educational Leadership and Administration*, two chapters for Sense publications on teaching with film and literary texts, and a forthcoming chapter, "Critical Policy/Practice," in *The Sage Handbook of Educational Leadership* (2nd ed.).

Tom Beech is president emeritus of the Fetzer Institute in Kalamazoo, Michigan. Formerly, he was CEO of the Burnett Foundation and The Minneapolis Foundation. He has served on the boards of the Council on Foundations and Independent Sector. Before entering the field of philanthropy, he was an executive with Apache Corporation.

Richard Bergeon is a principal of Bergeon, Fu and Associates. He holds a BBS in general management from Wayne State University, an MA in whole systems design from Antioch University, and certification as an organization systems renewal consultant. He has been employed as manager, director, and executive leadership consultant in banking, public utilities, transportation, manufacturing, pharmaceutics, and telecommunications. His specialties are adoption of new technologies and staff development.

Anne Berre received a BA in political science and English from Agnes Scott College and a JD from Emory University School of Law, both in Atlanta, Georgia. She practiced law in a large firm in the Midwest for twenty-six years while teaching as adjunct faculty and then joined the academy full time in 2005. Her current areas of research involve preparing young women to be the leaders of the future and alternative dispute resolution.

John Blenkinsopp is a reader (associate professor) in management at Teesside University Business School in the northeast of England. His research interests are largely in two areas—career management and development, and whistle-blowing and employee silence—and he frequently adopts a cross-cultural and comparative approach in his work. He is currently working on a European Commission-funded project examining the training and career development of medical physicists.

Juana Bordas is president of Mestiza Leadership International in Denver, Colorado. She is founder of MiCasa Women's Center and founding president of the national Hispana Leadership Institute. She has been vice president of the board of the Greenleaf Center and faculty member of the Center for Creative Leadership.

Skye Burn is executive director, The Flow Project, and fellow. She is UNESCO Chair for Comparative Studies of Spiritual Traditions, Their Specific Cultures, and Interreligious Dialogue, housed at the St. Petersburg Branch of the Russian Institute for Cultural Research, and board member, Center for Intercultural Dialogue, University of Oregon, home of UNESCO Chair for Transcultural Studies, Interreligious Dialogue, and Peace. She has a BA in psychology of the creative process, and an MA in leadership in social artistry.

Jay Gordon Cone is a senior consultant with Interaction Associates. He has spent the past twenty-five years focusing on leadership development and collaborative decision making. Jay served for five years as adjunct faculty for the executive MBA program at the University of Texas at Dallas. He holds a BA in philosophy from UCLA and an MBA from the University of Texas at Dallas. He is currently pursuing a PhD in organizational systems from Saybrook University.

Dennis Arthur Conners is an associate professor of leadership studies at Gonzaga University in the School of Professional Studies. Conners is also the founder and former director of the Leadership Formation Program in the School of Education at Gonzaga University. The Leadership Formation Program is an innovative program that prepares school- and district-level educational leaders. Conners's prime area of interest is in large and small systems transformation for social justice.

Phyllis A. Duncan is an assistant professor in the School of Business and Leadership at Our Lady of the Lake University, where she teaches in the Leadership Studies Doctoral Program. She has held various leadership positions in businesses including CEO, COO, and senior vice president. Phyllis holds an MBA from University of Arkansas, an MS in industrial engineering from Southwest University, and a PhD from University of the Incarnate Word. She can be reached at paduncan@lake.ollusa. edu.

Caroline Fu is assistant professor of the Doctoral Program in Leadership Studies at Gonzaga University. She holds a PhD in leadership and change and an MA in whole system design, both from Antioch University. Her MS in computer sciences and BS in applied mathematics, engineering (EE) and physics, are both from University of Wisconsin. She has a certificate of completion in system dynamics advanced study from the Sloan School of Management, Massachusetts Institute of Technology.

Mark Green is a retired military officer with assignments including the Pentagon and a tenured professor of leadership at Our Lady of the Lake University. He holds a PhD in educational administration and MS in information systems from the American University, an MBA from Our Lady of the Lake, an MEd from the University of Missouri, and is completing his MA in theology at Oblate School of Theology. He can be reached at Greem@ lake.ollusa.edu.

Tim Harle worked as an executive in both large corporations and SMEs: two threads running through his career have been leadership and change. He now writes, lectures, and consults using insights from complexity theory, ecology, and psychology. He is an associate consultant of Bristol Business School, United Kingdom, and a guest lecturer at IEDC Bled School of Management, Slovenia. A graduate of Cambridge University, Tim undertook advanced management studies at INSEAD. His website is www.timharle.net.

Laura M. Harrison is an associate dean of students at Stanford University and teaches in the Organizational Behavior and Leadership program at the University of San Francisco. Her research on advocacy and change has been published in the *Journal of Student Affairs Research and Practice*. Current projects include a National Association of Student Personnel Administrators grant-funded research project on effective advocacy and a chapter on transformational leadership in university settings, scheduled for publication in 2011.

Gill Robinson Hickman is currently a professor in the Jepson School of Leadership Studies at the University of Richmond. She has held positions as dean, professor of public administration, and human resource director. Her recent books include *Leading Change in Multiple Contexts* and *Leading Organizations: Perspectives for a New Era* (2nd ed.). Her current research and book projects focus on invisible leadership and leadership in socially active businesses.

Michael Jones is a leadership educator, writer, and pianist/ composer. He is the author of two books exploring leadership artistry and community and is also known for his many recordings of original compositions for solo piano. Michael is on the executive leadership faculties at The Banff Centre near Calgary, Alberta, and the University of Texas, San Antonio. He speaks on the relationship between leadership and creativity across North America. His Web site is www.pianoscapes.com.

Prasad Kaipa is founder and executive director of the Center for Leadership, Innovation and Change at the Indian School of Business. He also has been working as a coach and advisor to CEOs of a number of Fortune 500 companies for more than twenty years and previously was a manager and research fellow at Apple University.

Karen J. Lokkesmoe earned a PhD at the University of Minnesota in the Department of Education and Public Administration. Her dissertation, teaching, and consulting have focused on global leadership development, public and nonprofit management, and intercultural training. She was awarded the Global Leadership Dissertation of the Year Runner Up award from the Global Leadership Advancement Center for this research. She continues to consult and is adjunct faculty at Augsburg College in the Master of Arts in Leadership program.

James M. Mohr recently earned a PhD at Gonzaga University. His research interests include leadership, privilege, diversity, hate studies, and the process of othering. In addition, he has presented nationally and internationally on the interdisciplinary study of hate and privileged models of leadership. He is currently employed at the Community Colleges of Spokane and serves as the Chair of the Gonzaga Institute for Hate Studies.

Mark Nepo has published twelve books and recorded three CDs during the past thirty years. As a poet and spiritual teacher, he has taught extensively in North America and abroad in a wide range of settings. For eighteen years Mark taught at the State University of New York at Albany and for fifteen years served as a program officer for the Fetzer Institute in Kalamazoo, Michigan. In 2010, Mark sat down for an interview with Oprah Winfrey as part of her Soul Series on the SIRIUS satellite radio network. To learn more, visit www.MarkNepo.com and www.threeintentions.com.

Michael I. Poutiatine is an adjunct instructor of leadership studies at Gonzaga University in Spokane, Washington, where he teaches courses for both undergraduates and master's level students in leadership theory and practice. Poutiatine has a particular interest in the professional development of leaders in the field of education and in transformational leadership theory. He is also the principal partner in an educational research and consulting firm in Spokane.

Charles Salter is an assistant professor of business administration at Schreiner University. He teaches in the Doctorate of Leadership Studies for Our Lady of the Lake University, San Antonio. Charles holds a bachelor of journalism from the University of Georgia, an MBA concentration in management from University of Houston, an MBA concentration in finance from Western International University, and a PhD from Our Lady of the Lake University San Antonio. He can be reached at Salter16@hotmail.com.

Charles Torti is an associate professor and chair of the Business Department of Schreiner University. He teaches entrepreneurship, management, human resources, and business strategies in the School of Professional Studies. He attended North Texas State University and earned a master of business education. Charles holds a PhD in business administration from Touro University. He may be reached at cwtorti@schreiner.edu.

Eliane Ubalijoro is an adjunct professor at McGill University's Institute for the Study of International Development. She is also the founder and Executive Director for the Center for Leadership Excellence in Applied Research (C.L.E.A.R. International

Development Inc.) and an advisor to Rwandan president Paul Kagame.

Gilda Warden received a BSN from Pacific Lutheran University. Her master's in transforming spirituality and doctorate in educational leadership are from Seattle University. She works at Child Study & Treatment Center in Tacoma, Washington, and is adjunct faculty at the School of Health Sciences at Seattle Pacific University. She owns Sage Harbor retreats, classes, and seminars. Warden has lived in Panama, Guam, Brazil, and Japan, and various cities in the United States. She enjoys films and other cultural pursuits.

Rick Warm is a doctoral student in leadership and change at Antioch University and anticipates graduation in December 2010. He is the director of the Center for Wisdom in Leadership, an adjunct professor of leadership at Northern Kentucky University, and works as an executive coach and leadership consultant. Warm's career path has included work in organizations on five continents. His research focuses upon leadership education, wisdom, personal and organizational transformation, and the hero's journey.

Preface

Gill Robinson Hickman

Building Leadership Bridges (*BLB*) is an annual publication of the International Leadership Association (ILA). This volume, *Leadership for Transformation*, reflects a partnership among the ILA, the James MacGregor Burns Academy of Leadership, and the Fetzer Institute. The partnership formed as the result of a three-year grant awarded by the Fetzer Institute. Its purpose, as envisioned by the partners, was to help individuals understand the inner and outer aspects of leadership for transformation. Members of the partnership characterized *leadership for transformation* as, "people who play a pivotal role (often called leaders) in efforts (often called leadership processes) to achieve tangible and positive results in their organizations, communities, countries or the world—in a way that is collaborative, that is fueled by a contagious, empowering spirit, and that serves the common good" (T. F. Beech, personal communication, January 2, 2008).

The partners formed a stewardship team that would guide the project over a period of three years with members from each partner organization, including Mark Nepo, Deborah Higgins, and Megan Scribner from the Fetzer Institute; Carol Pearson, Judy Sorum Brown, and Michael Jones from the Academy of Leadership; and Cynthia Cherrey, Shelly Wilsey, and Gill Hickman from the ILA. The project, designed to deepen the understanding of and support the further development of theories concerning leadership for transformation around the world, was comprised of two interconnected elements: a series of retreats at Fetzer's Seasons Center and the 2009 ILA Global Conference on Leadership for Transformation in Prague. The retreats—on Transformational Leadership in Action, the Practice of Transformational Leadership, and the Nature and Dynamics of Transformational Leadership—each brought together different groups of leadership practitioners, educators, and scholars to discuss leadership for transformation from the perspectives of exemplars, practices, frameworks, or conceptual perspectives. Six hundred people from forty-six countries and more than two hundred organizations, businesses, and universities, furthermore, explored Leadership for Transformation at the eleventh annual ILA Global Conference in the dynamic city of Prague during the commemoration of the twentieth anniversary of the Velvet Revolution.

It is hoped that there will be three publications resulting from these collaborations, including *Transformational Thinking for 21st Century Leadership* (Carol Pearson, editor) and *Transformational Practices for 21st Century Leadership* (Judy Sorum Brown, editor). This first publication, *Leadership for Transformation*, synergistically emerged from the union of what the stewardship team informally called "the conference book" and the annual *BLB* publication. JoAnn Barbour, editor of *BLB*, and I joined forces to become coeditors of this innovative volume of work.

I am pleased that the book chapters and creative works in this unique volume give voice to some of the learning on transformational leadership that came from this partnership. We hope this volume will stimulate your interest in the topic and pique your curiosity for more exploration in the future.

Introduction

JoAnn Danelo Barbour and Gill Robinson Hickman

Leaders and participants can transform from many processes and ascribe a variety of interpretations to the meaning of a transformation, as in Kafka's *Metamorphosis*. In biology, we are all familiar with caterpillars turning into butterflies or tadpoles into frogs, those same frogs that, in folklore, shape shift into princes by enchantment. In folklore, additionally, one can be born a shape shifter and be transformed by natural forces, or shape shifters can be sorcerers or witches who have the ability to change at will (Yolen, 1986). In twenty-first-century reality television, for example, we see stars shape shift into dancers, "ugly ducklings" change into "swans," and common singers transform into idols. As we see evidence or allusions or illusions of transformation all around us, we hold that leadership for transformation is especially important. As Burns notes, "To transform something is to cause a metamorphosis in form or structure, a change in the very condition or nature of a thing, a change into another substance, a radical change in outward form or inner character" (Burns, 2003, p. 24).

When we posed several questions in the call for submissions for this first volume of *Building Leadership Bridges*, we wanted to know—since transformative change does not occur as the result of any one action by any one person and is the result of many acts, both large and small, carried out by many individuals in many locales—what are those acts, who are the actors, what is the process of leadership for transformation, and where and how does the process occur? We received ninety responses to the call, including transcripts of various Prague panels from the ILA's 2009 Global Conference. This volume, *Leadership for Transformation*, is an opportunity to share and learn about new research, effective leadership practices and proven teaching methods, and creative works that support the many faces of transformation. The authors in this volume present chapters from the arts to science, from qualitative to quantitative thinking, and about the leader transforming self to leaders for transformation. In this vein, we organize the chapters into theories or philosophies and worldviews, followed by practices or applications of transformation.

We begin the first set of chapters, Theory and Philosophy for Transformation, with a poem by Mark Nepo, one of five Nepo poems or brief meditations chosen for this volume. It is apropos that we begin a section of theory and philosophy with a reflective piece titled "The Practice before the Practice," since one has to think about his or her philosophy, worldview, values, and beliefs before leading for transformation. Next, Gilda Warden uses the philosophy of Hannah Arendt and the concept of natality to focus on leadership for transformation as innovative and full of potentiality. About beginnings, natality is a viable orientation for influencing change, according to Warden, who connects and explains natality with quantum leadership theory, healthy and toxic leadership, and renewal. A modern rethink of Taoist philosophy is discussed by Caroline Fu and Richard Bergeon, who describe how the Tao philosophy as a concept enables rethinking leadership and offers a process for assessing and guiding transformation. Because during a transformation, complexity and moments of aberration often cause digressions from intended outcomes, Fu and Bergeon offer the Tao Model as useful in navigating the perplexity. They present components of the Tao Model and translate those components to leadership for transformation. We transition from the Tao to fractals, as Tim Harle continues the theme of tensions and contradictions between individual and corporate, large and small, and local and global within a transformation process as he explores a framework that enables leaders to approach possible dualities using the concept of fractals from complexity theory. Harle holds, as does Warden, that the Newtonian worldview is not always the most appropriate model for leadership for transformation; he suggests that self-organization and emergence concepts of fractal leadership offer several implications for leadership practice.

A leader who has reflected upon philosophies and worldviews will begin to take action, and from the perspective of several authors, that action for transformation ought to be artistically grounded. We begin this section of the volume, Transformation Through Artistry, with a poem by Nepo, "Where No One Stays a Statue," and then continue philosophical grounding in the arts with lessons for leaders from improvisational theater. Because leaders are often creating, learning, and adapting as they go along, James Mohr holds that leaders ought to study improvisational theater to learn a deeper understanding of how to tap into one's creative, emotional, intellectual, physical, and spiritual cores to become better decision makers and more successful leaders during times of transformation. In his chapter, he shares six improvisational principles. Michael Jones, who provides a multi-artistic perspective, holds that in the future leaders will be remembered for their wisdom, empathy, presence, intuition, and artistry; thus, they need to be good artists who need to listen deeply to be attuned to the unheard melody emerging in the space between the musical notes. Jones discusses artistry from the perspective of the myths by which leaders live and suggests changing the light to develop a new set of guiding myths that he unfolds in his chapter. Leadership, continues Rick Warm, can be a developmental process about meaning and transcendence that is clearly a transformational journey. In his chapter, he explores the connection between the development of leaders and the hero's journey and argues that leadership requires personal transformation that will ultimately allow "leadership for transformation," a heroic journey that involves a quest for understanding and the search for meaning, a journey of change and transformation.

With the next set of chapters, Transformation in Practice, the focus turns from reflexivity to application. In these chapters, the authors discuss leadership knowing, the practice of learning the artistry of leadership for transformation, leadership research on transformational projects, or leading, that is, ways of practicing leadership for transformation. We begin the transition with a Nepo piece, "Wu Feng," a story about making choices. Jay Cone also talks about the importance of making choices: one can practice leadership either as a finite game for the purpose of winning or an infinite game played for the purpose of continuing the play. In his chapter, Cone discusses the different approaches, when, and how those approaches would or could be applied. He notes, for example, the worldview of a finite performer versus an infinite performer and makes some very insightful conclusions. From a research focus in the arts, Skye Burn reports on The Flow Project, wherein artists are engaged in a deep inquiry to identify principles of art and artistic practices common to the artistic experience across media. In addition to the mission of the project, to give leaders access to knowledge and experience that artists possess and give artists recognition for the value of their knowledge and experience, Burn discusses the process of this research project and findings, that is, what art can offer leadership.

From scholars observing artists in the studio as classroom, we shift to the academic classroom with Laura Harrison, who draws from her teaching experiences to propose a framework to teach leadership for transformation. She notes that students seemed to grasp the concepts more quickly in organizational theory and seemed to find leadership theory harder to understand at the practical level. Harrison proposes using critical pedagogical constructs to help with student understanding: ideology, hegemony, master narrative, and counter-narrative to study systemic power and transformational challenges in balancing social justice, political savvy, and self-preservation. From individual classrooms to classrooms within a program, Michael Poutiatine and Dennis Conners suggest that programs to develop school leaders must connect transformative learning theories with leadership practice. These authors discuss the theoretical framework used to teach leadership skills for effective and moral leadership and the will required for effective and socially just leadership, and they apply that theoretical base to a practiced model for preparing school leaders who live and practice social justice. They include a "virtual school" case simulation with debriefing and case analysis discussions.

Mark Nepo builds a bridge to the next section, Leadership for Transformation, with "The Work of the Worm," as we shift from studio and classroom applications of leadership for transformation to research in other arenas. John Blenkinsopp presents a case study of leadership that sought to tackle the problem of homelessness. He shows leadership for transformation, in part, through numerous acts of influence as he examines how leaders worked beyond organizational boundaries, building bridges with other stakeholders to effectively transform the lives of a particular section of society. Blenkinsopp found homelessness to be a multidimensional problem that requires an integration of public, private, and voluntary sectors on national, regional, and local levels.

As leaders communicate and influence others within the real world of the homeless, they must also communicate in the virtual world. Charles Salter, Anne Berre, Charles Torti, Mark Green, and Phyllis Duncan collaborated on a study to test the theoretical proposition that in a virtual environment there is a relationship between followers' personalities and their effects on followers' assessments of leadership behavioral style based on the word usage of the leader. They found that language is highly predictive of ratings of how transformational a leader is perceived to be, even when using virtual communication.

From a global perspective, Karen Lokkesmoe reports findings from a study on leadership in Brazil, India, and Nigeria, more specifically the perspectives and strategies that focus on developing countries and on public and nonprofit sectors. After discussing her findings from global leadership data gathered from a variety of grounded theory methods, Lokkesmoe presents an integrated model of global leadership development that consists of four competency domains global leaders must draw upon and an array of contextual factors that influence the conceptualizations and enactment of effective global leadership practice. Exploring leadership for transformation, Tom Beech, Juana Bordas, Prasad Kaipa, and Eliane Ubalijoro participated on a keynote panel at the 2009 ILA Global Conference in Prague, Czech Republic. The chapter in this volume is a written summary of the panel discussion moderated by Beech, who first introduced video segments featuring five world leaders, activists, and scholars. The panelists' discussion occurred within the context of the topics raised by the video clips and biographical work of the world leaders; topics included youthful idealism, indigenous people, Darfur, wisdom of the heart, and compassion. The goal of the session was to explore leadership for transformation from a range of perspectives, raise questions, stimulate conference participants' imaginations, and start conversations that would spill over into the rest of the conference and beyond. We end this volume of *Building Leadership Bridges* with a final reflection by Mark Nepo, "The Friendship of Tung-Shan and Yün-Yen," and with the hope that all readers of this volume of chapters about leadership for transformation find their truth.

Acknowledgments

While this volume would not be possible without the contributions of the authors, we especially express our appreciation to others who partner with us in this effort, helping in our own transformation. We are grateful for the work of Debra DeRuyver,

ILA director of membership services, who gently facilitated but strongly supported the process from individually submitted manuscripts to one cohesive volume of essays, and for Joanne Ferguson, a copy editor whose diligence helps transform all our efforts. Both Debra and Joanne make us all look good! Additionally, we thank members from the stewardship team who guided the "leadership for transformation" project over three years: Mark Nepo, Deborah Higgins, and Megan Scribner from the Fetzer Institute; Carol Pearson, Judy Brown, and Michael Jones from the Burns Academy of Leadership; and Cynthia Cherrey and Shelly Wilsey, respectively ILA's president and director. From the oft-quoted English poet Alexander Pope we sum our thoughts as editors: "The way of the Creative works through change and transformation, so that each thing receives its true nature and destiny and comes into permanent accord with the Great Harmony: this is what furthers and what perseveres" as we say a final thank you to the ILA Board of Directors for their continuing support and encouragement of our attempts to evolve in ways we hope will better serve all who study, practice, teach, and care about leadership in the world.

References

Burns, J. M. (2003). *Transforming leadership: A new pursuit of happiness.* New York: Atlantic Monthly Press.

Yolen, J. (Ed.). (1986). *Favorite folktales from around the world.* New York: Pantheon.

Leadership for Transformation

Theory and Philosophy for Transformation

The Practice Before the Practice

Mark Nepo

There is always a practice before the practice; a sitting before the incomprehensible long enough to feel and sometimes understand the mystery each instrument and craft is designed to invoke.

In Japan, before an apprentice can clay up her hands and work the wheel, she must watch the master potter for weeks. In Hawaii, before a young man can ever touch a boat, he must sit on the cliff of his ancestors and simply watch the sea. In Africa, before the children are allowed to drum, they must rub each part of the skin stretched over wood and dream of the animal whose heart will guide their hands. In Vienna, the prodigy must visit the piano maker before ever fingering a scale; to see how the keys are carved into place. And in Switzerland legend has it that before the watchmaker can couple his tiny gears, he must sit long enough to feel the passage of time.

Starting this way enables a love of the process that is life-giving. The legendary cellist Pablo Casals was asked at ninety-two why he still practiced four hours a day. He smiled and replied, "Because I believe I'm making progress."

It is this sort of deep progress that saves us.

Natality as Leadership
for Transformation

Orienting the Influence for Change

Gilda Warden

The notion of natality formulated by Hannah Arendt from her life experience during World War II in Europe is rarely heard of outside of philosophical literature and conferences. The word itself conjures up thoughts of pregnancy, babies, and mothers breast-feeding. Arendt, however, did not utilize the word in terms of embodiment; instead, she wanted to oppose the "miserable . . . desperate form of freedom, to live toward death instead of liking to live or instead of living for a cause" (Anders, 1948, p. 355). Arendt and the world witnessed the totalitarian leadership style of those whose nexus of action necessary for leadership to function was to destroy what they considered the untenable power of the Jewish people. Arendt's notion of natality provides a refreshing perspective in light of how mortality salience has both inspired and induced a defensiveness that is sometimes evident in leadership.

Arendt had been raised into German Enlightenment philosophy; she studied under Martin Heidegger at the University of Marburg in 1924 and later completed her dissertation, *Love and Saint Augustine*, under the direction of Karl Jaspers in 1926 (Disch, 1994). As Hitler rose to power, Arendt shifted from academia to become a political and historical thinker, resisting National Socialism and even experiencing arrest (Disch, 1994, p. 16). Arendt was among the myriad artists, intellectuals, musicians, philosophers, and writers who with her husband and mother were able to escape to the United States through the assistance of American journalist Varian Fry in 1941.

Arendt was convinced that those who were duped into thinking that there was some auspiciousness to entertaining cooperation with the Nazis were incapable of sustaining her conviction that the norms of conventional humanism were sufficiently ample to guarantee what she called "the reality of the public realm" against unparalleled human violence (Arendt, Baehr, & Baehr, 2003, p. 204). Regarding the theme of leadership for transformation, I propose that Arendt's notion of natality is a viable orientation for influencing change. I first consider how contemporary quantum leadership is transformational leadership and lends itself quite well to the concept of natality. Second, a review of mortality salience is necessary for two reasons: the extent to which the scholars in leadership studies have spent time considering the writings of Heidegger, Otto Rank, Ernest Becker, and others is evident in the theories behind what motivates both healthy and toxic leadership. Finally, I examine natality as the position from which both leadership and the renewal of leaders can be expressed most fluently.

Transformational and Quantum Leadership

Leadership for transformation implies a paradigmatic shift, a new way of influencing others toward a kind of leadership no longer based on the Newtonian "people as machines" model (Porter-O'Grady & Malloch, 2007). Quantum theory indicates relationships between particles; in a leadership for transformation setting, quantum leadership is interpreted as leaving behind the isolative task achievements as sole metrics of performance. In other words, where there is relationship and sharing of new information, transformational leadership is the method for new energy to do the work. Quantum transformational leaders attend to the ebb and flow as well as to the interchange of energy among the leaders' constituents (Wells, 2009).

As we transition away from the Industrial Age, a different shift is occurring: Whereas in the past, shifts were seen soon after the fact, the unfolding of future changes will be too brief to allow us to make plans to accommodate them; so leaders are both change agents and are changing themselves at virtually the same time as they perceive change (Porter-O'Grady & Malloch, 2007, p. 7). The crux of quantum transformational leadership consists of linear thinking being replaced by relational and whole systems thinking; structure will be about wholes, not parts (p. 13). Keep in mind that the universe as a whole is in a constant fluctuation characterized by both permanence and change (Morgan, 2006). Order is natural, emergent, and free; its precise nature can never be planned or predetermined (p. 256). Mutual causality cultivates "systemic wisdom" that encourages the development of mind-sets and skills that focus on recognizing and changing patterns (p. 272). We must remember that a quantum leader who wants to be transformational needs to approach the organization being led from a very different point of view: The leader must shun transformation strategies that amount to merely restructuring current arrangements and instead fashion an innovative system that allows people to contribute to their fullest potential; and there can be no suggestion of asserting control in the traditional sense (Porter-O'Grady & Malloch, 2007, p. 313).

Mortality Salience in Leadership

In the current worldview experienced through all the gifts of media, our lives are filled with continual reminders of our own mortality. Because we do not wish to die, individually or communally, many of us utilize our leaders as saviors; that is, because we feel helpless in the face of chronic anxiety about our present and future well-being, we rely on those leaders who give us a sense of safety and hope. Under the protection of our leaders, death will be kept at bay and we can continue to live our lives in the illusion of a death not immanent. In some situations, toxic leadership prevails, meaning that the followers or constituents of toxic leaders are powerless under the control of those who have such a fear of death themselves that precarious leadership skills are used to create the illusion of safety.

We must be reminded of the context within which Arendt lived. She was aware that the concentration camps were places that people were existentially dead but not yet annihilated. Their inhumane segregation created a sense of the inhabitants having departed from the world yet were not announced as dead; those in the camps were tortured in such a calculated way so as to promote dying without death occurring (Villa, 2007). Arendt wrote in *The Human Condition*: "We are perhaps the first generation which has become fully aware of the murderous consequences inherent in a line of thought that forces one to admit that all means, provided that they are efficient, are permissible and justified to pursue something defined as an end" (1998, p. 229).

Felman and Laub (1992) provide another perspective to the culturally persistent memory of the Holocaust. They note that "death has taught a lesson that can henceforth never be forgotten. If art is to survive the Holocaust—to survive death as a master—it will have to break, in art, this mastery which insidiously pervades the whole of culture and the whole of the aesthetic project" (p. 33). Totalitarian leaders are servants of inhuman forces, bearing no responsibility for the processes they set in motion (Canovan, 1992). Those who felt they were heroic in their terrible actions transmuted their fear of death into the security of self-perpetuation, obviously to the point of facing up to death and even courting it in order to propagate their superior race (Becker, 1973/1997).

Without consideration or analysis of what makes a leader toxic, let us take into account the possible transforming of toxic leaders who have been diminished by their time in shadows. Low emotional intelligence, inequalities, humiliating and degrading policies, slipshod leaders who sweep conflict under rugs, and multiple-dysfunctional-people-situations all comprise toxic relationships that develop in poor systems in which tyrants are protected or directed (Goldman, 2009). In his recently published work, *Transforming Toxic Leaders*, Goldman offered multiple principles for moving any organization from toxicity to stunning performance. Among his many recommendations are to use narratives to build a collaborative culture, use small-wins strategies, and adopt a language and culture of abundance (p. 126). Each of these approaches interrupts the harmful environment sanctioned by a toxic leader.

Natality as Orientation for Change

Consider what we have looked at so far: quantum leadership as transformative and mortality salience as a nexus for leadership behavior. It is important in exploring Arendt's notion of natality that we consider the context: Her views are greatly influenced by her experiences of the totalitarian regime sweeping over Europe that terrorized millions under the guise of taking economic power away from the Jews and promoting the purity of the Aryan race. This of course is a simplification of the quite complex motivation behind the insane leadership of Hitler. What Arendt knew about, however, was dying people not yet dead; this crime against humanity was perpetrated against Arendt's own people and to others the Nationalists somehow considered inferior: Gypsies, homosexuals, Jehovah's Witnesses, Russian prisoners of war, the handicapped—the list of innocents goes on. In response to German refugee Eric Voegelin, who had considered astonishing Arendt's belief that a "change in human nature" was possible, Arendt replied, "The success of totalitarianism is identical with a much more radical liquidation of freedom as a political and as a human reality than anything we have ever witnessed before. Under these conditions, it will hardly be consoling to cling to an unchangeable nature of man and conclude that either man himself is being destroyed or that freedom does not belong to man's essential capabilities. Historically we know of man's nature insofar as it has existence, and no realm of eternal essences will ever console us if man loses his essential capabilities" (Arendt, as cited in Young-Bruehl, 1982, p. 254).

Years later Arendt wrote *The Human Condition,* which surprisingly did not speak explicitly to the "Jewish problem" or the concentration camps or to the extermination of millions. Instead, she did what literary critic Harry Berger called the "conspicuous exclusion" of themes that are "saturatingly present" in great texts or artworks, but only as silence or *felt absence* (Villa, 2007, p. 93). The "important and concrete discussions . . . carried by another dimension . . . become 'light' in all their reality" was what her mentor Karl Jaspers wrote in response to the book (p. 94). In *The Human Condition,* Arendt introduced "The Vita Activa," which was comprised of labor, work, and action. Whereas labor and work comprise the biometabolic life processes and the "artificial world of things," action is what goes on between and among human beings or the "plurality" of the human condition (Arendt, 1998, p. 220). Speech and action are what make humans human because those actions are performed among other humans (Arendt, 1998, p. 176). It is through speech and action that we are individuated and we reveal our distinctiveness and singularity. To act means to take initiative, to begin, to put something into motion (p. 177). We see here how those who were "dying yet not dead"—among other interpretations of the horror of the concentration camps—were existentially no longer human (Villa, 2007, p. 98).

The fascination with beginnings that assert the notion of natality is evident in Arendt's dissertation, *Love and Saint Augustine* (Arendt, 1996). Through Augustine's highlight on "entering the world through birth" as a precondition of freedom, Arendt is able to challenge Heidegger's notion of mortality as the foundation of action (p. 146). Arendt had the beginnings of a consciousness that we are shaped fundamentally by the conditions of our births, by our community into which we are born, and by "The Neighborhood"—the last regards neighborly love which in Arendt's dissertation is the most foundational of Augustine's three concepts of love (Young-Bruehl, 1982, p. 75). In *The Human Condition*, Arendt provided a numinous interpretation to one's beginnings:

> The miracle that saves the world, the realm of human affairs,
> from its normal, "natural" ruin is ultimately the fact of natality,
> in which the faculty of action is ontologically rooted. It is, in
> other words, the birth of new men and the new beginning, the
> action they are capable of by virtue of being born. Only the full
> experience of this capacity can bestow upon human affairs faith
> and hope, those two essential characteristics of human
> existence which Greek antiquity ignored altogether,
> discounting the keeping of faith as a very uncommon and not
> too important virtue and counting hope among the evils of
> illusion in Pandora's Box. It is this faith in and hope for the
> world that found perhaps its most glorious and most succinct
> expression in the few words with which the Gospels announced
> their "glad tidings": A child has been born unto us. (Arendt,
> 1998, p. 247.)

Arendt earlier acknowledged that mortality is the most certain law and the "only reliable law" between birth and death; nevertheless she believed that our lives would be spent in ruin if this law of mortality were ". . . not for the faculty of interrupting it and beginning something new, a faculty which is inherent in action like an ever-present reminder that men, though they must die, are not born in order to die but in order to begin" (Arendt, 1998, p. 246).

Because we are born, we have within us the desire to begin. We can be called beginnings or *natals*. By being born to begin, Arendt is giving us all the hope that second chances provide; she also reminds us that because there are new people being born all the time, new ideas, thoughts, and plans are also available all the time. This elegant concept implies leadership for transformation, including recognition of our equality as humans because of our experiencing beginning, being born.

Theologian Elizabeth Moltmann-Wendel considered Arendt's notion of natality as a clarion call for Western civilization that has fastidiously held on to the concept of mortality as the springboard for all our actions and decisions. Moltmann-Wendel noted, "Instead of being set on the linear and inevitable end of our life in death, we could use our being born as a never-ending desire for a new beginning and surprise as an orientation. With each birth, something new comes into the world. This worldview can again steer our view to the desire for life which stood at our very beginning" (Moltmann & Moltmann-Wendel, 2003, p. 54). If we consider our trajectory from birth "to move along a rectilinear line in a universe where everything, if it moves at all, moves in a cyclical order," Arendt named that a mortality orientation (Arendt, 1998, p. 19). That straight-line thinking may not acknowledge the diversity in our midst, and if there is an obstacle, such as a person who looks, prays, or loves differently than my normative, that obstacle must be diminished so as to not have ever existed; we know of peoples, cultures, or coworkers who are silenced or invisible to those single-minded ambitious ones who persist to climb the ladder, move ahead, not look behind, become the head of a division, not caring who was used as a means to the end result. Something along the way that makes life bearable is the strength of narrative. It was when we did not know the people behind the concentration camp fences, when they were so isolated from the rest of humanity that they ceased to exist except for the bored SS who guarded them, when they became out of sight, out of mind; these instances of nonbeing were interrupted when individual stories of Holocaust experiences became public. Arendt believed that "human essence . . . can come into being only when life departs, leaving behind nothing but a story" (1998, p. 193). When her dear friend and mentor Karl Jaspers died, Arendt spoke at his funeral:

We do not know, when a man dies, what has come to pass. We know only: he has left us. We depend upon his works, but we know that the works do not need us. They are what the one who dies leaves in the world—the world that was there before he came and which remains when he has gone. What will become of them depends on the way of the world. But the simple fact that these books were once a lived life, this fact does not go directly into the world or remain safe from forgetfulness. That about a man which is most impermanent and also perhaps most great, his spoken word and his unique comportment, that dies with him and thus needs us; needs us who think of him. Such thinking brings us to a relationship with the dead one, out of which, then, conversation about him springs and sounds again in the world. A relationship with the dead one—this must be learned, and, in order to begin this, we come together now, in our shared sorrow. (Arendt, as quoted in Young-Bruehl, 1982, p. 422)

Natals die; yet it is in the living between natality and mortality that we create our stories. In leadership for transformation, it is in how we influence others for change that we center our stories of beginning anew every day. Of the myriad ways in which we can interrupt the damages that incur through our acts in the world, forgiveness is what Arendt considered the most likely way to begin anew. She noted, "Trespassing is an everyday occurrence which is . . . constant establishment of new relationships . . . and it needs forgiving, dismissing . . . only by constant willingness to change their minds and start anew again can they be trusted with so great a power as that to begin something new" (Arendt, 1998, p. 240). Renewal in leaders, necessary to ensure healthy organizational and worker capacities, is based on the notion of natality. In our humanity as leaders, we become weary of being watched, imposed upon, needing to make important and urgent decisions at the drop of the hat, not to mention working more hours in a week than is appropriate for leisure and sleep to balance out our lives. Because we come to these places of wilting, we must recognize the signs and symptoms of pending toxic behavior or of a suffering constituency under poor leadership. When leaders recognize the pitfalls in leading, self-correction can take place; we can improve our self-learning abilities, reflect on the meaning of life and the spiritual strengths available to those who of us who seek them; we can certainly take up an extracurricular cause that will balance out the stressors from work. The notion of natality tells each leader to begin again and again and again in care for his or her self to ensure the continuity of care for the organization and individuals within it.

Natality as Leadership for Transformation

Natality serves as a refreshing perspective from which to derive a transformative leadership outlook. In consideration of Arendt's notion of natality in light of the context from which the notion was derived, in light of quantum leadership that is transformative in nature, and in light of natality as a lens through which a leader considers the new, renewal, and rebirth, let us finally consider leadership as innovative and provisional of potentiality.

Considering innovation as that which creates the new, which converts knowledge and ideas into benefit, or what brings extrinsic recognition (Porter-O'Grady & Malloch, 2007), let us also add again that natality is interruptive of the status quo. To interrupt the status quo would require risk taking; natality, then, as an orientation for change would require a leader no longer playing it safe but instead challenging the past to a better future through not just inspirational phrases but inspirational behavior, actions that motivate others by demonstrating what can be accomplished through candor and vulnerability, appreciating small wins, and supporting risk taking by others as well as permitting success and failure (p. 207).

Natality is an orientation for transformative leadership. It comes from a place that few of us reflect upon, the miracle of our beginning, the actuality of being; of living as not just mortals but also as natals. Let us celebrate the possibilities involved with leading from a stance of the new. With Hannah Arendt providing the context for the notion of natality, let us be conscious of her gift of insight, of knowing how to provide a new beginning for all of our ways of influence, yet most of all for the imperative and timely necessity of beginning, as natality, as an orientation to influence change.

References

Anders, G. A. (1948). On the pseudo-concreteness of Heidegger's philosophy. *Philosophy and Phenomenological Research*, 8(3), 337–371.

Arendt, H. (1996). *Love and Saint Augustine*. (J. V. Scott & J. C. Stark, Eds.). Chicago: University of Chicago Press. (Original work published 1929)

Arendt, H. (1998). *The human condition* (2nd ed.). Chicago: University of Chicago Press. (Original work published 1958)

Arendt, H., Baehr, P., & Baehr, P. R. (2003). *The portable Arendt*. New York: Penguin Books.

Becker, E. (1997). *The denial of death*. New York: Simon & Schuster. (Original work published 1973)

Canovan, M. (1992). *Hannah Arendt: A reinterpretation of her political thought*. New York: Cambridge University Press.

Disch, L. (1994). *Hannah Arendt and the limits of philosophy*. Ithaca, NY: Cornell University Press.

Felman, S., & Laub, D. (1992). *Testimony: Crises of witnessing in literature, psychoanalysis, and history*. New York: Routledge.

Goldman, A. (2009). *Transforming toxic leaders*. Palo Alto, CA: Stanford University Press.

Moltmann, J., & Moltmann-Wendel, E. (2003). *Passion for god: Theology in two voices*. Louisville, KY: Westminster John Knox.

Morgan, G. (2006). *Images of organizations*. Thousand Oaks, CA: Sage.

Porter-O'Grady, T., &. Malloch, K. (2007). *Quantum leadership: A resource for health care innovation* (3rd ed.). Sudbury, MA: Jones & Bartlett.

Villa, D. (Ed.). (2007). *The Cambridge companion to Hannah Arendt* (4th ed.). New York: Cambridge University Press.

Wells, C. (2009, June). *Leadership, quantum mechanics, and the relationship with professional learning communities*. Retrieved from: http://cnx.org/content/m24349/1.1/.

Young-Bruehl, E. (1982). *Hannah Arendt: For love of the world*. New Haven, CT: Yale University Press.

A Tao Model

Rethinking Modern Leadership
for Transformation

Caroline Fu and Richard Bergeon

The whole world—cultures, organizations, and individuals—focuses increasingly on transformation. Every leader, whether prior to or in the throes of transformation, hopes to achieve intended results successfully with minimal thrashing. This chapter describes how the Tao, as a concept, enables rethinking leadership and offers a process for assessing and guiding transformation.

Our concept, based on the Tao philosophy, draws upon modern physics and our reflections on leading transformations in organizations and teaching the Tao of Leadership in a doctoral program. The Tao philosophy, rooted in ancient Chinese cosmological science about nature's phenomena, is an attempt to inspire leadership transcendence in dealing with change. In the ancient cosmology, we found abstractions addressing notional aspects of change and a meta-pattern for successful transformations that are scientifically explainable. Integrating the Tao concept with the meta-pattern resulted in a proposition that we call the "Tao Model."

The model can assist scholars and practitioners to find order in incomprehensible leadership phenomena. Just as increasing complexity gave birth to Confucianism, which sought to cultivate societal order in contrast to the Tao emphasis on embracing nature's spontaneity (Capra, 1975/1991), neither dismissed the other but sought harmony. The model augments and corroborates the existent leadership theories to bridge practice and theory, helps demystify the theoretical and philosophical underpinnings of transformation, and supports leadership practice and development. Using the model may increase clarity and deepen thoughts in applications.

Underpinnings of the Tao Model

The Tao Model (C. Fu, 2008) delves into a less obvious realm of transforming leadership. The model comprises a theoretical and conceptual scheme for probing beyond behavioral observables to an unseen source of transformation: energy-flow. The concept of energy-flow came from Chinese philosophy, cosmological science, and modern physics. Energy-flow is an abstraction of process flow of energy in a spatiotemporal field of relationships.

Burns unwittingly described energy-flow in his description of the leadership *initiator*. The initiator "takes the first step toward change. . . . She breaks the ice. And what is this act? To communicate with other potential actors in order to gain a positive response" (Burns, 1998, p. 12). Burns's initiator links back to Einsteinian physics: energy is a (quantum) abstraction of concrete facts in thought, a "reflective correspondence with [the] 'real thing'" (Bohm, 1980, p. 53). For example, concrete events perceived as physical activities transform into energy retained in our thoughts as "sense perceptions" (Einstein, 1922/1956, p. 2). Energy-flow is the biological basis for physical and mental activities such as our thoughts and feelings. Emerging from those thoughts is a view that transformation involves social interactions that may be described using energy-flow abstractions to comprehend the full range of human experiences, including leadership phenomena.

Perceiving and enfolding (Bohm, 1980) the idea that energy-flow is an abstraction evokes a relativistic view of social life. We often associate sudden realizations or epiphanies with igniting a lightbulb; this image is not too far from reality, as energy-flow travels at lightning speed from neuron to neuron to form human perceptions. Einstein proved macroscopic (material and mass) energy transforms into microscopic (quantum) energy when it travels at the speed of light. Using $E = mc^2$ (Einstein & Infeld, 1938/1966), Einstein averred, "Everything is energy." Thus transformation of energy, to or from matter/mass, is an energy-flow abstraction in nature. Our ability to contrast matter and energy in physics provides the foundation for contrasting material and energy-flow as forces in social life (Russell, 1938). Whitehead, an Einstein contemporary, linked energy-flow with social life when he contrasted materialism with another abstract form of social energy—the spiritual. Whitehead (1925/1953) observed, "Both the material and the spiritual bases of social life were in process of transformation" (p. 101). Because there is a division between the material and spiritual perceptions of social life, he hoped the transformation would lead the world to "the notion of energy being fundamental, thus displacing matter [or material] from that [base] position" (p. 102). Thus, energy and spiritual bases form "a uniform way of dealing with circumstances" of social life (p. 202).

Jung related physics and social life to Chinese thought: "The ancient Chinese [sage's] mind contemplates the cosmos in a way comparable to that of the modern physicist, who cannot deny that his model of the world is a decidedly psychophysical structure" (Wilhelm & Baynes, 1950/1997, Foreword by Carl G. Jung). Engaging in a relativistic view of social life, the ancient Chinese sages believed that cosmic energy-flow (known as Super Cosmic Ch'i) affected inspiration, environment, and social interactions on Earth. They provided a symbol to visualize the total abstraction of "being" and constancy of change in all nature's phenomena—the 5,000-year-old Tai-Ji (☯) symbol. The literal translation of Tai-Ji is "Great Supreme" (P. Y. Fu, 1953, Ch. 1), or the universal energy-flow of consciousness. Now commonly referred to as the "Tao" symbol, it signifies the Universal

Substance (Secter, 1993, p. 20). The intertwining black-white areas represent the polarities seen in nature, that is, day/night, light/dark, and hot/cold. The oppositely colored dots within each represents the existence of complementarities (Siu, 1957/1971) embraced by each polarity. The yin and yang rotate and transform into each other—expressing variations of "being"—having no beginning and no ending (P. Y. Fu, 1953), affecting Earth as formless Super Cosmic Ch'i. The cosmic ch'i interacts with each individual's personal "ch'i" amalgamating personal energy-flow with the universal consciousness. Ch'i is the nature and consequence of being, energy-flow, and transformation.

According to an ontological assumption of Chinese cosmological science, ch'i is an energy-flow activated by unity and creative tension within the apparent dualities of the intrinsic-extrinsic. This creative tension can be viewed as a "creative urge dipolar" (Whitehead, 1929/1967, p. 332) relationship between the elemental yin and yang energies. Those energies are in continual motion, like Earth's rotation in the solar system, manifesting as night/day and season cycles. The different polar intensities of interacting energy-flow, ch'i, induce the dynamics underpinning the epistemological power of nature's primary energies. If "we keep to the physical idea of energy: then each primordial element will be an organised system of vibratory streaming of energy" (Whitehead, 1925/1953, p. 35).

The polarity creates both attracting and repelling forces, which induce magnetic energy-flow interactions. The polarity of yin (- -) and yang (—) is akin to a binary language (0, 1) used in computer processing. The Chinese ancient sages developed a language to communicate the nuances in social life using eight symbols to represent permutations of energy-flow in nature. The eight symbols, called *trigrams*, represent various state manifestations: Heaven (☰), Earth (☷), Mist (☱), Thunder (☳), Mountain (☶), Wind (☴), Water (☵), and Fire (☲). They each have attributes distinct from, yet contain some aspect of similarity with, each of the others. They make available a symbolic language that represents all nature's phenomena and human affairs (Siu, 1968/1972).

Leadership as an energy-flow concept is a relativistic abstraction that provides a useful set of references for leading transformation to meet different circumstances with different attributes of energy-flow. The preceding theoretical grounding for using energy-flow abstractions touches upon some aspects of social life. Combining the original ancient trigrams with the leadership as energy-flow theory, we can introduce a set of meta-order energy-flow abstractions.

The Tao Model of Leadership for Transformation

Ancient Chinese sages, philosophers, and theorists earned respect for their contributions to leadership practice. The *Book of Changes*, *I-Ching*, developed as a guide for leaders and their advisors (Siu, 1968/1972; Wilhelm & Baynes, 1950/1997), reveals cosmic wisdoms for dealing with nonobvious dynamics underlying the obvious that leaders subsume and resonate (Siu, 1978, p. 84). Through *I-Ching*, we learned the language and some meta-patterns of flow among the trigrams that the ancient leaders used to find order in the incomprehensible complexity of leadership. After delving into more than thirty *I-Ching* translations, and the original Chinese recording, we saw that a set of leadership for transformation labels coalesced.

The Tao Model provides a framework for leaders to continually reflect on the present, explore potentials, and anticipate both changes and decisions in a transformation. Table 2.1 illustrates correlations between the *I-Ching* trigrams, leadership energy-flow, and the ensuing effect on leadership. The columns from left to right show: nature's trigram energy-flow labels and symbols, translation in modern science language, the labels selected to represent the leadership energy-flow abstractions, and a synthesis of leadership processes involved in transformation (C. Fu, 2008, p. 33).

Table 2.1 Converting from Nature's Energy-Flow to Leadership Energy-Flow

Trigrams	Symbolic Representations of Energy-Flow	Leadership Energy-Flow	Effect of Energy-Flow on Leadership
Heaven	Symbolizes oneness, determination, majesty, and high principles Generates field of universal energy that are spiritual and ethical mind forces protecting all within its sphere of influence	Founding	Creates a foundation, kernel, and locus, concurrently, from which to defend or transform
Earth	Represents the manifestation of essence, dynamically at rest, completely free of pressure and tension, open, and nourishing Has no personal agenda; rather, forms a substantive cohesive collection of individual particulars and an assembled multiplicity	Sustaining	Sustains original creation, nurtures growth, creativity, and development of multiple disciplines Maintains well-being of the collective whole
Mist	Stands for the unanticipated, unknown, and lurking dangers while being mysterious Evaporates subtly upward while settling downward forming oceans and lakes Delights the cold-hearted and destroys the unwary negligent	Innovating	Invokes fresh, untested, unknown ideas that appear dangerous, yet is curiously attractive and enticing Ventures into places where no one known has ever been before
Thunder	Characterizes lightning and sound moving quickly in multiple directions while being in multiple places simultaneously Rebounds quickly traveling in straight lines that form an interior angle that produces a resonating chamber in which the material and spiritual blend	Responding	Responds to internal issues and challenges swiftly Provides multiple resolutions Stimulates others to action and plants seeds for actionable ideas

Element	Description	Role	Description
☶ Mountain	Embodies metaphysical beginning and ending—a symbol of action at rest and an immobile gateway to inner spirit. Brings to question any movement that would cause disruption	Anchoring	Anchors fresh ideas to the collective purpose of existence and core values. Provides a cornerstone or foundation rock, self-assured and introspective; sometimes subtle and nonobvious
☴ Wind	Depicts advancing and retreating constantly, a most cerebral, unpredictable, changeable energy. Finds ways to move around curvaceously, quickly, and slowly with the capacity to simultaneously envelope and penetrate, often in ways that are comfortable and caressing	Influencing	Invites charismatically and influences suavely while yielding or compromising when appropriate. Permeates convincingly and turns the populace into believers, with or without hidden agendas
☵ Water	Connotes erosion of canyons, abysses, caverns, and dry river beds, always falling, tumbling, flowing, streaming, swirling unpredictably down and around. Contains within the expressed confinement of a heart and soul in the locked within body, unfulfilled yearning	Strategizing	Meanders and deals diligently and continuously through circuitous obstructions and environments. Creates new paths with a mission, abiding by policies purposefully
☲ Fire	Represents sudden and incredible bursts of energy moving slowly forward and upward while consuming everything in its path, including destructing self. Brings clarity of consciousness, intuitive awareness, resistant on the outside and yielding within	Implementing	Brings forth bright, sociable, enlightening, impassioned attributes. Arouses those on whom it depends to do work within the prescribed route in spite of the ultimate purposes

SOURCE: The Symbolic Representations of this column 2 is adapted from Secter (1993), pp. 24–31. Copyright 2008 by C. Fu.

Table 2.1 indicates that there are varying degrees of yin-yang energy-flow states in nature corresponding to those in human affairs. We mimicked the ancients to represent leadership attributes. Each leadership energy-flow has its unique and shared aspects for performing specific functions to achieve the collective aspiration. The order, from founding to implementing, suggests a meta-order energy-flow of leadership related to transformations.

Following, we list the meta-order leadership energy-flow attributes linearly. As a precursor for embarking on transformation, leaders must have a transforming vision, identifying gaps between current reality and desired future.

1. *Founding* creates the base for a transforming leadership vision.
It is about leadership energy needed to establish a foundation on solid ground before a transformation starts, such as ensuring there is clear vision and available resources for accomplishing the transformation.

2. *Sustaining* provides and facilitates receptive leadership.
It is about leadership energy required to sustain foundation solidity, to hold and support all functions throughout the transformation effort, such as acquiring, developing, and maintaining staff capacity.

3. *Innovating* leadership brings about joyous ideal and collective happiness.
This energy is about innovative leadership and other transformational ideas that could lead people into a desired future, such as conceptualizing groundbreaking ideas for a new process, product, and/or service.

4. *Responding* leadership arouses inquiry and offers feedback.
This energy is about provoking multidirectional communications; offering feedback, critique, and advice about intended and/or unintended outcomes; consulting is involved at each level of leadership function.

5. *Anchoring* leadership keeps intact adhering to values and purpose.

This energy is about ensuring a transformation is grounded and adheres to people's wants and needs and the organization's core values and purposes; this leadership energy provides the cornerstone of the transformation foundation.

6. *Influencing* leadership uses gentle persuasion to share a vision.

This energy is about spreading the transformation initiative, reaching out to every corner of the organization to communicate the vision, elicit participation of the collective in transforming the organization.

7. *Strategizing* leadership sets direction navigating through turbulence.

This energy adheres to the global transformation purpose, defines locally the strategic directions for tactical implementation to achieve local goals within the global purpose of the transformation.

8. *Implementing* leadership lights and guides the path.

This energy is about keeping tactical activities focused on the set strategy; it guides and assists people to perform the detailed tasks required to accomplish the transformation successfully.

The progressive energy-flow is cyclic. One can start anywhere in the flow to assess, diagnose, or plan the next action step in a transformation. Each energy-flow state in a transformation affects all other states: "Counting that which is going into the past depends on the forward movement. Knowing that which is to come depends on the backward movement" (Wilhelm & Baynes, 1950/1997, p. 265). Thus, leaders might skip backward to rectify an unresolved situation or forward if the conditions of the situation are well in hand.

To illustrate the interactive dimension of the cyclic and temporal aspects of energy-flow transformation, the ancient sages derived the "Inner-World Arrangement" (Wilhelm & Baynes, 1950/1997, p. 269) from traces of nature's cosmic energy-flow. The left box of Figure 2.1 shows that arrangement of the Super Cosmic *Ch'i*. The arrows represent the flux, temporality, and

Figure 2.1 Inner-World Arrangement

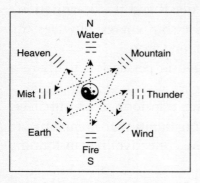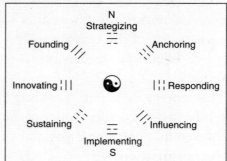

SOURCE: Copyright 2008 by C. Fu.

intensity of energy-flow, known as the cosmic "fly-through" pattern (Too, 2000, p. 59). The right box, retaining that ancient arrangement, replaces the traditional trigram labels with our leadership energy-flow labels.

Figure 2.2, derived from the ancients' universal cosmic energy-flow, is finite. The curvy arrows indicate how the eight leadership energy-flow abstractions intermingle, exchange, and transform. The energy-flow movements subsume and resonate with the Tao consciousness at the center, creating a transcendent virtuous leadership path from the prior energy-flow state to the next.

The energy-flow pattern is a meta-order. Although it may appear as a sequential and discrete-stepwise process, it is nonlinear. One may jump back and forth in thoughts, as in virtual presences, to envision or reinvent the future, to design or redesign the transformation. In the real world of transformation, leadership energy-flow may physically manifest at different places and form into increasingly complex patterns. It is likely several transformations may be going on at the same time to make the underlying pattern even more complicated and obscure. During transformations, certain parts of the process could be iterative, recursive, and overlap states of other efforts; a transformation

Figure 2.2 Synchronizing with Meta-Order Energy-Flow: The Tao Way for Leading Transformation

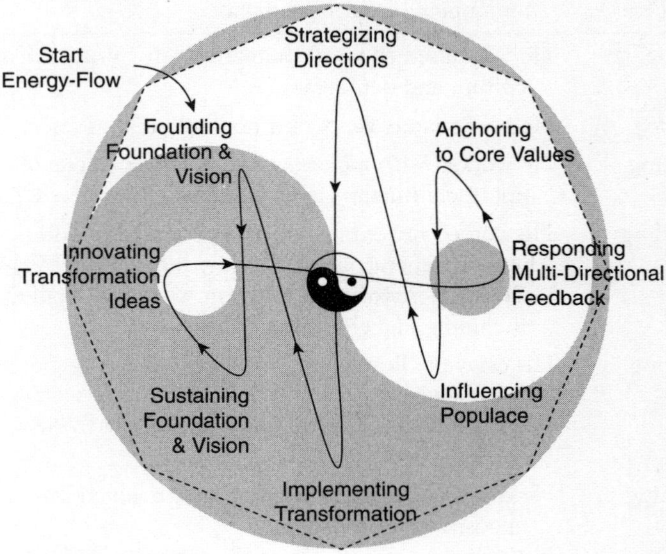

SOURCE: Copyright 2008 by C. Fu.

flow may become very complex and difficult to discern. Organizational resources, cultures, traditions, behaviors, and external influences all contribute to the formation of unique flow-patterns and layers at the reality level.

Using the Tao Model

Many great transforming leaders evidenced the presence of energy-flow in their transformation efforts. Burns (2003) included the historical incidences of several (C. Fu, 2008). We find energy-flow in the transformation enlightenments of great spiritual leaders. Their everlasting legacy continues to stimulate intellectual and spiritual thought.

To illustrate how to find energy-flow in a contemporary transformation effort using the model, we selected the Czech

**Table 2.2 Energy-Flow of Václav Havel's Leadership
for Transformation**

Energy-Flow	Transforming Leadership Instance
Founding	He was raised to honor humanitarian values of Czech culture and democracy.
Sustaining	He passionately supported nonviolent resistance.
Innovating	He worked with a close group of others to create an apolitical human rights manifesto known as Charter 77.
Responding	He worked toward restoration of quashed reforms. The government punished many influential Czech and Slovak signatories in different ways, some jailed including Havel himself.
Anchoring	His essay of "Post-Totalitarianism" (*Power of the Powerless*), exposes mistaken values, the social and political order that enabled people to "live within a lie."
Influencing	He cofounded a support group that evolved into an opposition movement. He played a leading role in the reform, achieving international notoriety by working with the Communist Party, ultimately winning the party's confidence.
Strategizing	During the Velvet Revolution, the opposition led by Havel worked with the Communist government to negotiate reforms leading to the formation of a democracy. Ultimately, the parliament elected Havel president of the country.
Implementing	His thirteen years in office saw radical change in his nation, including its accession into NATO and the negotiations for membership in the European Union, completed in 2004.

Republic's past president, Václav Havel (1936–). (See Table 2.2.) Though only history can witness transformation sustainability, Havel's leadership in the nonviolent revolution, resulting in the Czech Republic's democracy, satisfies Burns's acid test. This acid test offers "a potent equation: embattled values grounded in real wants, invigorated by conflict, empowered leaders and activated followers to fashion deep and comprehensive change in the lives of people" (Burns, 2003, p. 213). The following is a brief summary and analysis of Václav Havel's leadership abstracted from the Internet:

> Havel was originally not a politician, but a playwright and essayist, raised to honor humanitarian values of Czech culture. Beginning in the 1960s, his work turned to focus on the politics of Czechoslovakia. When the Warsaw Pact intervention in Czechoslovakia in 1968 ended the Prague Spring, a reformist period, Havel decided to work toward restoration of quashed reforms. He published his essay of "Post-Totalitarianism" (*Power of the Powerless*), describing the modern social and political order that enabled people to "live within a lie." He worked with a small group to create an apolitical human rights manifesto known as Charter 77. The government punished the many Czech and Slovak influential signatories in different ways, some jailed including Havel. He cofounded a support group that evolved into an opposition movement. Havel played a leading role in the reform movement achieving international notoriety by working with the communist party, ultimately winning the party's confidence. During the Velvet Revolution, the opposition led by Havel worked with the communist government to negotiate reforms leading to the formation of a democracy. Ultimately, the parliament elected Havel president of the country. His thirteen years in office saw radical change in his nation, including the Czech accession into NATO and negotiations for membership in the European Union later completed in 2004. (Havel, 2004)

In that example, the analysis of Havel's transformation effort, his vision, and sounding and sustaining energies are implicit in the leadership lens. The explicit energy-flow began with the innovating energy-flow of transforming the Czech Republic government and people. Havel's leadership, characterized by nonconfrontation and cooperation, worked to the benefit of the Czech people, and his example may serve as a guide for others.

Another example of a transformational leader that has withstood the judgment of history is Milton S. Hershey (1857–1945), a confectioner, philanthropist, and founder of The Hershey Company (see Table 2.3).

> Milton Snavely Hershey saw the value of philanthropy. His love and continuing support for the betterment of humanity through business success in confections set the stage for future establishments. Through his business acumen, he became a confectioner pursuing perfection in the art of candy making. Hersey ultimately became widely known for high quality candy and use of the freshest ingredients. Moving his production into the midst of local dairy farms near his birthplace, Hershey watched the community thrive. Seeing the success of both company and community as linked, his sense of perfection led him to take responsibility for the prosperity of employees and the company town. He always placed the quality of his product and the well-being of his workers ahead of profits. In 1903, he began construction on what was to become the world's largest chocolate manufacturing plant. His vision turned to philanthropy starting with a resident school for orphans. He formed many trusts and foundations, and gave the school's trust control over The Hershey Company and other foundations so that his goodwill would be perpetuated long after his demise. (Brenner, 2000)

Table 2.3 Energy-Flow of Milton S. Hershey's Leadership for Transformation

Energy-Flow	Transforming Leadership Instance in Business and Nonprofit Initiatives
Founding	He demonstrated philanthropy and business acumen.
Sustaining	His love and continuing support for the betterment of humanity through business success in confections set the stage for future establishments.
	He always placed the quality of his product and the well-being of his workers ahead of profits.

Table 2.3 *Continued*

Energy-Flow	Transforming Leadership Instance in Business and Nonprofit Initiatives
Innovating	Through trial and error in perfecting manufacturing, he created his own formula for milk chocolate, using the latest mass production machinery techniques. Seeing the success of both company and community as linked, his sense of philanthropy led him to take responsibility for the prosperity of employees and the company town.
Responding	Hersey ultimately became widely known for high-quality candy and use of the freshest ingredients. In 1903, he began construction on what was to become the world's largest chocolate manufacturing plant.
Anchoring	Hershey transferred the majority of his assets, including control of the company, to the formation of the Milton Hershey School Trust, to benefit the Industrial School, allowing it to keep control of the company and his philanthropy ideal. He endowed his entire fortune to building the town of Hershey and Hershey Industrial School.
Influencing	He formed many trusts and foundations and gave the school's trust control over The Hershey Company and other foundations so that his goodwill would be perpetuated long after his demise.
Strategizing	He moving production into the midst of local dairy farms near his birthplace and developed his business as well as the community. His vision and strategy was building a complete community around his factory.
Implementing	Hershey's support, houses, businesses, churches, and a transportation infrastructure accreted around the plant. He established the M. S. Hershey Foundation, Hershey Entertainment and Resorts Company, Hotel Hershey, Hershey Park, Hershey Museum and Hershey Gardens, the Hershey Theatre, and the Hershey Community Archives. Milton Hershey School Trust founded the Penn State Hershey Medical Center, a teaching hospital with an annual budget exceeding the initial construction cost.

Both leadership examples conformed to Burns's acid test (Burns, 2003). Havel and Hershey illustrated bettering humanity through their leadership in transforming people collectively by working for the benefit of the people. Those examples may serve as a guide for public, business, and not-for-profit leadership.

Conclusion

During a transformation, complexity and moments of aberration often cause digressions from intended outcomes. People often become confounded. The Tao Model is useful in navigating through the perplexity. Utilizing such a transformation analysis can assist leaders to discern undergirding dynamics; enable them to respond effectively to unanticipated stimuli and complexity; and render an ability to assess, comprehend, and avoid making unintended costly decisions. The Tao Model provides a way for assessing the status of a transformation, determining whether there are overlooked stages or elements, and guiding the transformation to its culmination.

The Tao Model provides a means for creating the common playing field, a transcendent space for leaders to think about the elements of transformation. It presents a simple vocabulary or shorthand for communication of status and intent. The energy-flow frame of reference invokes creative ideas for tackling difficult situations and transforming conflicting forces into complementarity. It holds promise for becoming a widely used model for developing leaders and rethinking leadership for transformation.

References

Bohm, D. (1980). *Wholeness and the implicate order*. London: Routledge.

Brenner, J. G. (2000). *The emperors of chocolate: Inside the secret world of Hershey and Mars*. New York: Broadway.

Burns, J. M. (1998). Empowerment for change. In *Kellogg Leadership Studies Project: Rethinking Leadership*. College Park, MD: Burns Academy of Leadership Press.

Burns, J. M. (2003). *Transforming leadership: A new pursuit of happiness*. New York: Grove/Atlantic.

Capra, F. (1991). *The Tao of physics: An exploration of the parallels between modern physics and eastern mysticism* (3rd ed.). Boston: Shambhala. (Originally published/written 1975)

Einstein, A. (1956). *The meaning of relativity, including the relativistic theory of the non-symmetric field* (5th ed.). Princeton, NJ: Princeton University Press. (Originally published/written 1922)

Einstein, A., & Infeld, L. (1966). *The evolution of physics, from early concepts to relativity and quanta*. New York: Simon & Schuster. (Originally published/written 1938)

Fu, C. (2008). *Energy-flow—A new perspective on James MacGregor Burns' transforming leadership: A new pursuit of happiness*. Doctoral dissertation, Antioch University, Yellow Spring (OhioLINK ETD: http://rave.ohiolink.edu/etdc/view?acc_num=antioch1218205866).

Fu, P. Y. (1953). *Philosophy of Chuangtse*. Thesis, National Taiwan University, Taipei.

Havel, V. (2004). In *Encyclopedia of world biography* (Vol. 7, pp. 202–205). Detroit: Gale Virtual Reference Library.

Russell, B. (1938). *Power: A new social analysis*. New York: Norton.

Secter, M. (1993). *I Ching clarified: A practical guide*. Rutland, VT: Charles E. Tuttle.

Siu, R. H. G. (1971). *The Tao of science: An essay on Western knowledge and Eastern wisdom* (Vol. 1). Cambridge, MA: MIT Press. (Originally published/written 1957)

Siu, R. H. G. (1972). *The portable dragon: The Western man's guide to the I Ching* (Vol. 2). Cambridge, MA: MIT Press. (Originally published/written 1968)

Siu, R. H. G. (1978, Spring). SMR Forum: Management and the art of Chinese baseball. *Sloan Management Review, 19*(3), 83.

Too, L. (2000). *Practical feng shui formulas for success*. Boston: Element.

Whitehead, A. N. (1953). *Science and the modern world*. Toronto: Collier-Macmillan Canada. (Originally published/written 1925)

Whitehead, A. N. (1967). *Process and reality, an essay in cosmology*. New York: Macmillan. (Originally published/written 1929)

Wilhelm, R., & Baynes, C. F. (1997). *The I Ching or Book of changes* (R. Wilhelm, Trans.). Princeton, NJ: Princeton University Press. (Originally published/written 1950)

Fractal Leadership

Emerging Patterns for Transformation

Tim Harle

Contemplating a flock of birds or a shoal of fish, some might ask, "Where is their leader?" (YouTube, 2008). A flock or shoal is contrasted with traditional examples of leadership: an orchestra has its conductor, an army its general. But do such notions of leadership resonate in a world that is at once connected and disconnected (Friedman, 2006)? From music to the military, notions of leadership are changing.

The debate about leadership for transformation often involves tensions, if not contradictions, between the individual and the corporate, the large and the small, the local and the global. In this chapter, I explore a framework that enables us to approach such dualities using a concept from complexity theory: fractals. Fractals in nature demonstrate repeated patterns that can be observed at different levels in a system. This observation provides a framework for exploring the suggestive notion that we might see repeating patterns in leadership at different levels. Individual and corporate, large and small, local and global: transformation can be encouraged through consistent, repeating patterns of leadership.

In approaching the concept of fractal leadership, I explore two key themes from complexity theory: self-organization and emergence (Holland, 1998). I examine the significance of boundaries in living systems, discuss patterns of both consistent and inconsistent leadership through a number of organizational examples, and explore the implications of a fractal approach for leadership practice, noting its coherence with business ethics. In reflecting critically on an emergent approach to leadership, I address a major challenge with illustrations from the history and literature of the past century and then draw some conclusions for leadership practice.

Living Systems and Boundaries

A view of organizations as living systems is not new. De Geus (1997) wrote of the living company, and Morgan (2006, pp. 33–69) includes the organism as one of his images of organization. For Barrett (1998, p. 66), the organization is a living entity, whose physical, emotional, mental, and spiritual well-being needs to be cared for. Conversely, we can still read that "corporations, of course, are not biological" (Brown, 2005, p. 4). Wheatley, one scholar who has addressed the significance of boundaries, writes that "complex networks of relationships offer very different possibilities for thinking about self and others. The very idea of boundaries changes profoundly. Rather than being a self-protective wall, boundaries become the place of meeting and exchange. We usually think of these edges as the means to define separateness . . . But in living systems, boundaries are something quite different. They are the place where new relationships take form, an important place of exchange and growth" (2005, p. 48). The significance of boundaries and the need to manage context was identified by Gosling and Mintzberg (2003). The worldly mind-set is one of five managerial mind-sets they propose; it resonates with the approach we explore for leadership that spans the local to the global: "To manage context is to manage on the edges, between the organization and the various worlds that surround it—cultures, industries, companies" (p. 60).

Insights from Complexity Theory: Self-Organization and Emergence

Insights from complexity theory challenge the dominant Western view of leadership, a Newtonian world of cause and effect.

Complexity theory has been applied to a wide range of fields. Of particular interest to the leadership debate are the applications of complexity theory to strategy (Levy, 1994), leadership (Wheatley, 1999), organizational studies (Stacey, Griffin, & Shaw, 2000), systems thinking (Hoverstadt, 2008), and organizational change (Olson & Eoyang, 2001). Beinhocker (2006) provides a startling perspective on economics, Sweeney and Griffiths (2002) offer new insights on health care, and Morrison (2002) addresses school leadership. Other applications include geography and the social sciences (Byrne, 1998), postmodern philosophy (Cilliers, 1998), and ultimate questions of life and meaning (Gregersen, 2003).

Emergence and self-organization challenge notions of direction and control (Streatfield, 2001). As Cisco's cross-functional business councils found, "For a company used to *making* things happen, it is very hard to convert to *letting* them happen" (Moore, 2006, p. 50, italics original). A new perspective is offered by *U.S. Marine Corps Doctrinal Publication* 6 (1996), which describes command and control as "a process of continuous adaptation" (quoted in Meyer & Davis, 2003, p. 152). Additionally, contemporary military strategy speaks of Mission Command (*Auftragstaktik*), which seeks "to empower even the most junior commanders to grasp the moment and capitalise fleeting opportunities without the need for specific permission" (Burridge, 2007, p. 99).

Reflecting on the pioneering work of biologists Maturana and Varela, Wheatley (in Wheatley & Kellner-Rogers, 1996, p. 49) reminds us that "we can never direct a living system. We can only disturb it." This means that the common expression "change management" has an oxymoronic ring, though Malik (2004) describes managing change in the context of fractal dynamics. This observation about living systems is disturbing to some, liberating to others. Lewin and Regine (1999) provide an illustration of the former: "Witness the reaction of one manager who was attending a seminar by Ralph Stacey . . . [who] was urging his audience to embrace uncertainty, to give up tight control, and to allow for unpredictability, when someone in the audience wailed, 'You have just set management back fifteen or twenty years!'" (p. 50f.).

Stacey and his colleagues offer an ongoing challenge to those venturing into this field. Building on Kantian philosophy and Mead's social psychology, they "examine the claims made by management complexity writers. Do they hold out the potential for a radical re-examination of how we think about organizations; that is, re-examination that goes to the very roots of our thinking? Or are they but the latest in the explosion of management fads we have seen over the past few decades, another superficial fashion that leaves untouched the roots of management thinking and so soon fades? We argue that a great many writers run the fad risk" (Stacey et al., 2000, p. 2). A key distinction, highlighted by Griffin (2002, p. 124), is that between systemic self-organization and participative self-organization. Agents—in our case, especially leaders and followers in interrelationships—cannot stand outside the system but are part of it. Their behavior and interactions help co-create the future.

Wheatley echoes Stacey's challenge about control and links it with another key feature of complexity theory: emergence. "Fearing people, we control one another mercilessly. Fearing change, we choose our little plans over the surprise of emergence" (Wheatley & Kellner-Rogers, 1996, p. 94). The concepts of self-organization and emergence are brought together by Pascale and colleagues: "Self-organization in business relies on intelligence that exists in every part of a complex adaptive system (in the mind of every employee) and makes it possible to tap this resource and release its formidable potential. That capacity, in turn, allows companies to seize opportunities and solve problems as they arise. Self-organization and emergence are the twin engines of adaptive work" (Pascale, Millemann, & Gioja, 2000, p. 120).

One aspect of emergence deals with how small interactions create large-scale patterns: a swooping flock of birds is a commonly quoted example. Traditionally, an organization's culture has been seen as something that was driven "top down," yet recent authors offer a different perspective. Harrison's (2007) autobiographical account of the agency staff industry is subtitled *How Small Gestures Build Great Companies.* Badaracco (2002) emphasizes the ordinary situations that define quiet leaders. Neither uses the language of complexity theory, but both accounts are entirely in accord with its precepts, especially that of participative self-organization and emergence, where a whole system demonstrates features that emerge from its constituent agents. The observations of Harrison and Badaracco about the widespread impact of small actions provide an entry to the debate on global and local leadership, but the debate begs a question.

Global and Local: A False Dichotomy?

Be global. Be local. Can complexity theory provide insights that help to conceptualize transformational leadership? Small interactions and large-scale patterns invite us to examine the concept of fractals: repeating patterns in nature observed at different levels. The term *fractal* was coined by Benoît Mandelbrot in the mid-1970s (see, for example, Mandelbrot, 1982). Prompted by an investigation into the length of Britain's coastline and observations of unexpected patterns emerging from random generation software, he recognized self-similar patterns that occur at different levels in a system. (Note that levels form an inherent part of a systemic perspective without inexorably leading to some of the constraints associated with traditional notions of hierarchy in an organization.)

Some challenge the application of fractals, questioning the idea of deterministic chaos (see Boulton & Allen, 2007, p. 226, citing Cilliers, 1998). The proliferation of computer-generated fractal images offered via the Internet tends, ironically, to reinforce a mechanistic view. But with our focus on living systems, it is naturally occurring patterns that provide a vivid window into the world of leadership. In particular, the idea of repeating patterns at different levels provides a helpful conceptual framework for studying global and local—or worldly (Gosling & Mintzberg, 2003)—leadership.

Fractals in an Organizational Context

Fractals offer a distinctive framework for studying organizations— from global corporations to small communities—while viewing them as complex adaptive systems. How can front-line workers expect to behave in one way if their supervising board or individual managers behave in another? How can managers promote teamwork if performance management systems encourage individual reward? We should expect to see repeating patterns, fractals, at different levels.

An early business application of fractals was to the area of strategy (Zimmerman & Hurst, 1993). Levy (1994) speculated that "similar patterns of behavior might be expected whether one examines competition between countries, between firms in an industry, or even between departments in a firm" (p. 173). A recent study notes an (unacknowledged) fractal pattern: "The system of strategy . . . works at every level we've studied, from top corporate strategies through individual plans" (Logan, King, & Fischer-Wright, 2008, p. 231).

Stacey (1995) provided a link to leadership, using a complexity perspective to pose the question: "How useful is the distinction between the tactical and the strategic in a world in which undetectable tiny actions can escalate into major outcomes, making it impossible to say in advance whether an action is tactical or strategic?" (p. 492). Intel provides an illustration. According to company legend, Andy Grove and Gordon Moore were discussing what business they should be in. "Grove asked Moore what they would do if Intel were a company that they had just acquired. When Moore answered, 'Get out of memory,' Grove suggested that they should do just that. It turned out, though, that Intel's revenues from memory were by this time only 4% of its total sales. Intel's lower level managers had already exited the business. What Intel hadn't done was shut down the flow of research funding into memory (which was still eating up one-third of all research expenditure). Nor had the company announced its exit to the outside world" (Bower & Gilbert, 2007, p. 75).

Olson and Eoyang (2001, pp. 108–114) propose a methodology for organizational change based on the metaphor of fractals. They suggest the same patterns of behavior or relationship appear in multiple places and times across the organization. Examples of fractal self-similarity include dress, norms of behavior, habits, and company traditions. Shared values, perspectives, and standard operating procedures also demonstrate self-similarity between levels and across functional areas.

Fractal Leadership

Wineberg, who highlights the importance of consistency throughout an organization, has developed the concept of fractal leadership (2005, p. 29). A sustained application of fractals to leadership (Easum, 2000, pp. 99–105) originates in a faith community, where consistency is presumably an admired characteristic. Taking an evolving approach to language where nouns become verbs, Easum summarizes succinctly, "Leaders fractal" (2000, p. 105).

Even where there is no acknowledgment of fractals, we can observe repeating patterns described positively. One is revealed by that totem from the 1990s corporate toolkit, the balanced scorecard. An unnamed company "found significant correlation between employees' morale . . . and customer satisfaction. . . . Customer satisfaction, in turn, was correlated with faster payment of invoices" (Kaplan & Norton, 1996, p. 84).

Some authors make an explicit link to fractals. To Hurst, "a strategy . . . must also be present at all levels in the organization"

(1995, p. 166). Olson and Eoyang (2001) demonstrate from a complexity theory perspective that they understand the importance of small events and repeating patterns. They note that a complex adaptive system "always has some similarity at all levels of the system—individual, group, organization. . . . Thus learning about a system on one level provides information about all of the other levels. For example, different departments in the same organization will share values, procedures, or communication habits. . . . You will seldom find an immaculate coffee area on one floor and a filthy one on another" (Olson and Eoyang, 2001, p. 105).

Brian France, chairman and CEO of NASCAR, found a simple way to implement the company's value of teamwork: "We gave everyone a business card, from the janitor to the CEO" (Logan et al., 2008, p. 167). The same study found that Gordon Binder, former CEO of Amgen, credits his time in the U.S. Navy with learning the importance of values and vision: "If you walk on board a ship and the brass is polished, the guns will shoot straight" (Logan et al., 2008, p. 217). Sometimes inconsistencies are unearthed, as UPS found when it sought to create an airline: "Pilots wanted to be addressed by other UPS employees as 'Captain' even though the CEO and other top managers of the company went by their first names like everyone else" (Brewster & Dalzell, 2007, p. 82f.). These examples illustrate how emergence and fractal leadership—consistent behavior in small interactions, repeated at different levels—provide a helpful conceptual framework for addressing leadership.

Implications for Leadership 1: Where Is Leadership Situated?

A fractal approach can be applied to various aspects of the leadership agenda. We examine two. First, where is leadership situated? A fractal view accords with advocates of distributed, or dispersed, leadership (Raelin, 2003). As the contrasting examples of companies such as Southwest Airlines and Enron illustrate, corporate culture and leadership are interwoven (Tourish & Vatcha, 2005). The CEO and first-line supervisor should demonstrate consistency; the subject matter of their work might vary, but a repeating (fractal) pattern should be observable. Responsibility is shared.

Ritchie and Deakin Crick (2007) applied distributed leadership to the educational sphere, drawing a parallel with the individual needs of learners. Coining the term "living leaders" for the "ordinary heroes" they observed in their research, Binney, Wilke, and Williams (2005) note that "leaders are not just at the top but in the middle of a complex network of relationships. Living leaders recognise this interdependence" (p. 242).

Kelly, Iszatt White, Martin, and Rouncefield (2006) offer a thought-provoking perspective on leadership and learning. Their conclusion, drawing attention to Alvesson and Sveningsson's (2003) "extra-ordinarization of the mundane" accords with the importance of messy everyday interactions. Badaracco (1997), writing as a business ethicist, notes the importance of everyday decisions and actions, where people get their hands dirty.

A thoughtful contribution to situated leadership is provided by Simpson and French, who suggest, "In the current organizational context of radical uncertainty, the ability to lead demands precisely the capacity to tolerate ambiguity, uncertainty and complexity in the present moment. When the pressure is on, however, to meet targets based exclusively on the measurement of outputs, the 'default' position tends to be *control*" (2006, p. 254, italics original). Simpson and French add that "negative" capacity will tend to be ignored or pass unnoticed and will eventually atrophy (the linguistic parallel with living systems is striking). They conclude that at both the macro and micro levels we should focus on "leading by concentrating our minds on the present moment, as the place where *new knowledge may emerge*" (2006, p. 254, italics added). Note the parallel with a complex adaptive system yielding emergent properties not observable in its constituent parts.

Implications for Leadership 2: Ethical Leadership

A second application of fractal leadership is in the area of ethics. Griffin (2002) has applied to ethics a complexity perspective, including emergence and participative self-organization. A fractal view of leadership sees consistency at all levels, from local to global (Harle, 2009). Fractals reflect this consistency. Ethical behavior can then be seen as an emergent property, evolving from the relentless consistency of leaders at all levels.

As with ethics, so with an organization's values. Values, according to a former senior executive, "were central at Southwest Airlines, but they just happened" (quoted in Gittell, 2003, p. 226). Do organizational shared values "just happen," or should we decide up front what they will be? Who should decide the patterns of ethics in an organization? Western organizations cling to an outmoded view I have characterized as Newtonian: If those at the top of organizations mandate sound ethical values, then ethical behavior will result. Such cause-and-effect thinking is exemplified in a variety of organizational codes of ethics and regulatory regimes. From ancient codes such as the Ten Commandments to the Sarbanes-Oxley Act, the implicit worldview is, If these behaviors are mandated (cause), then appropriate behavior will follow (effect). But, as Pascale (1999) notes, "An important and distinct property of living systems is the tenuous connection between cause and effect" (p. 92).

The radically different emergent approach to leadership offers an alternative explanation both to the values that are so demonstrable at Southwest Airlines and the nature of ethical leadership. Far from "just happening," values and ethical behavior can be viewed as emergent properties, evolving from the relentless consistency of leaders at all levels, even though Garratt (2003) notes, "The US, despite all the current post-Enron rhetoric, is still stuck in a compliance-only time warp" (p. 136).

The best guard against unethical behavior is not subscription to a code of ethics, nor externally mandated frameworks, but relentless consistency of approach, fractals of ethical behavior. An emergent view emphasizes the importance of consistency in small interactions, rather than "set piece" pronouncements.

Given the bad press managerialism generally receives (for a more sympathetic view, see Poole, 2008), it is interesting to note that support for a fractal approach to leadership is provided by Enteman (1993). He describes his book on managerialism as "in a sense . . . a prolegomenon to business ethics" (p. 218). "We can securely locate business ethics as a function in the organization. Its primary location should be in the planning process itself. The best organization will not face a constant barrage of ethical questions" (p. 219). Although a complexity theorist would want to challenge the focus on planning, consistent leadership behavior promotes both the conditions for self-organization and the emergence of values. Business ethics is now seen as an integral part of an organization rather than some separate activity.

Challenges to Emergent Leadership

A fundamental challenge to fractal leadership needs to be addressed. An emergent approach to leadership may result in a consistency, a repeating fractal pattern that does not constitute a moral good (Harle, 2009). William Golding, in *Lord of the Flies* (1954), provides a chilling challenge to those promoting self-organization and emergence. On a broader scale stands Nazi Germany (Kellerman, 2008, pp. 97–124). Emergence and the potential of small events put a different perspective on the "small humiliations" tolerated in the early 1930s (Kellerman, 2008, p. 100). Grint (2005) offers a further challenge: How do advocates of distributed leadership respond to the rise and persistence of al-Qaeda? (pp. 143ff.).

The response to this challenge to the moral efficacy of fractal leadership is grounded in a feature running through our exploration, that of boundaries and ecosystems. Leadership involves managing at the edges (Gosling & Mintzberg, 2003). Viewing organizations from the perspective of living systems highlights the importance of disturbance for healthy ecosystems. "Relentless discomfort is a discipline that arrests the drift of living systems toward self-confirmation and homeostasis" (Pascale et al., 2000, p. 258). In particular, we need disturbance across boundaries. Although the events of *Lord of the Flies* occurred on an island, corporate history also reveals examples where disturbance from within has promoted healthy ecosystems (Harle, 2007). UPS founder Jim Casey coined a term to describe a "compulsive habit of tinkering with the status quo: 'constructive dissatisfaction,' which managers actively encouraged" (Brewster & Dalzell, 2007, p. 45). Sir Stuart Rose, who is credited with the turnaround of Marks and Spencer, "talked about the need for 'restless dissatisfaction'" (Bevan, 2007, p. 287).

Grint (2005) describes a helpful guard against such trends in relationships between leaders and followers: constructive dissent. Grint uses examples from the Royal Air Force (RAF) leadership courses for senior noncommissioned officers; his idea has been taken up by a senior RAF officer (Burridge, 2007): another fractal pattern?

Toward Conclusions

We may begin to draw some conclusions from the application of a fractal model to leadership. First, the implicit Newtonian worldview that underlies much thinking about organizations does not always provide the most appropriate model for leadership. In particular, we can challenge whether the "cause and effect" paradigm behind corporate initiatives, from change programs to codes of conduct, is likely to generate long-lasting embedded behaviors.

Second, participative self-organization offers a worthwhile model for exploring leadership. Central to the notion is the fact that traditional ideas of control must be discarded. Disturbance is more appropriate than direction. New ways of learning need to be embraced. Participative self-organization offers significant challenges to existing processes for identifying, developing, and sustaining leaders (Bolden & Kirk, 2009).

Third, leaders' everyday small actions are vital. Leaders can help to create an environment in which sustaining values—customer service, financial health, patient care, staff commitment, innovation, quality—emerge.

Fourth, the consistency of everyday actions leads to repeating patterns, fractals, that leaders at all levels demonstrate. The results, while different in detail, exhibit demonstrable similarities. Leaders of global corporations can be local leaders. In a complementary way, fractal leadership in an organization leads to consistency in that organization.

Fifth, fractal leadership reinforces a helpful approach to ethics. Consistency in leadership encourages the emergence of repeating patterns of behavior, fractals.

Sixth, fractal leadership is congruent with a number of recent approaches to leadership, including distributed or dispersed leadership and quiet leadership.

Last, disturbance is crucial to the health of organizations. Transformational leaders have a responsibility to promote it.

Summary

Gosling and Mintzberg (2003) observe that "'globalization' sees the world from a distance, assuming and encouraging a certain homogeneity of behavior" (p. 59). Questioning whether homogeneity is what we want from our managers, they correctly note that "a closer look reveals something rather different. Far from being uniform, this world is made up of all kinds of worlds" (p. 59). In this chapter, we have explored fractal leadership as a conceptual framework that not only takes account of the ecosystems of all kinds of worlds in which leaders operate but also offers "consistency" as a healthier alternative to homogenization. This radically different approach offers both an alternative insight into the nature of leadership and an alternative explanation to the values that are so demonstrable in some world-leading organizations. Emergence and self-organization offer leaders—whether operating at a global or local level, or anywhere in between—a profound perspective to embrace an approach through which consistency leads to repeating patterns: fractals. Fractal leadership can enhance our understanding of transformational leadership because the very unpredictability inherent in complexity theory prevents its domestication.

References

Alvesson, M., & Sveningsson, S. (2003). Managers doing leadership: The extra-ordinarization of the mundane. *Human Relations, 56,* 1435–1459.

Badaracco, J. L., Jr. (1997). *Defining moments: When managers must choose between right and right.* Boston: Harvard Business School Press.

Badaracco, J. L., Jr. (2002). *Leading quietly: An unorthodox guide to doing the right thing.* Boston: Harvard Business School Press.

Barrett, R. (1998). *Liberating the corporate soul: Building a visionary organization.* Boston: Butterworth Heinemann.

Beinhocker, E. D. (2006). *The origin of wealth: Evolution, complexity, and the radical remaking of economics.* Boston: Harvard Business School Press.

Bevan, J. (2007). *The rise and fall of Marks and Spencer . . . and how it rose again.* London: Profile Books.

Binney, G., Wilke, G., & Williams, C. (2005). *Living leadership: A practical guide for ordinary heroes.* Harlow, UK: FT Prentice Hall.

Bolden, R., & Kirk, P. (2009). African leadership: Surfacing new understandings through leadership development. *International Journal of Cross Cultural Management, 9,* 69–86.

Boulton, J., & Allen, P. (2007). Complexity perspective. In M. Jenkins, V. Ambrosini, & N. Collier (Eds.), *Advanced strategic management: A multiple perspective approach* (pp. 215–234). Basingstoke, UK: Palgrave.

Bower, J. L., & Gilbert, C. G. (2007). How managers' everyday decisions create—or destroy—your company's strategy. *Harvard Business Review, 85*(2), 72–79.

Brewster, M., & Dalzell, F. (2007). *Driving change: The UPS approach to business.* New York: Hyperion.

Brown, M. T. (2005). *Corporate integrity: Rethinking organizational ethics and leadership.* Cambridge, UK: Cambridge University Press.

Burridge, B. (2007). Action-centred leadership in the Royal Air Force: Final landing or new horizon? In J. Gosling, P. Case, & M. Witzel (Eds.), *John Adair: Fundamentals of leadership* (pp. 95–108). Basingstoke, UK, and New York: Palgrave Macmillan.

Byrne, D. (1998). *Complexity theory and the social sciences: An introduction.* Abingdon, UK, and New York: Routledge.

Cilliers, P. (1998). *Complexity and postmodernism: Understanding complex systems.* Abingdon, UK, and New York: Routledge.

de Geus, A. (1997). *The living company: Growth, learning and longevity in business.* Boston: Harvard Business School Press.

Easum, B. (2000). *Leadership on the otherside: No rules, just clues.* Nashville, TN: Abingdon.

Enteman, W. F. (1993). *Managerialism: The emergence of a new ideology.* Madison and London: University of Wisconsin Press.

Friedman, T. L. (2006). *The world is flat: A brief history of the twenty-first century, release 2.0.* New York: Farrar, Straus & Giroux.

Garratt, B. (2003). *The fish rots from the head.* London: Profile.

Gittell, J. H. (2003). *The Southwest Airlines way: Using the power of relationships to achieve high performance.* New York: McGraw-Hill.

Golding, W. (1954). *Lord of the flies.* London: Faber & Faber.

Gosling, J., & Mintzberg, H. (2003). The five minds of a manager. *Harvard Business Review, 81*(11), 54–63.

Gregersen, N. H. (Ed.). (2003). *From complexity to life: On the emergence of life and meaning.* New York: Oxford University Press.

Griffin, D. (2002). *The emergence of leadership: Linking self-organization and ethics.* London and New York: Routledge.

Grint, K. (2005). *Leadership: Limits and possibilities.* Basingstoke, UK, and New York: Palgrave Macmillan.

Harle, T. (2007). The prairie and the rainforest: Ecologies for sustaining organizational change. *Business Leadership Review, 4*(3), 1–15.

Harle, T. (2009, April). *Take me to your leader: Towards a fractal view of ethical leadership.* Paper presented at 13th European Business Ethics Network UK Conference, Bristol, UK.

Harrison, S. (2007). *The manager's book of decencies: How small gestures build great companies.* New York and Cambridge, UK: McGraw-Hill.

Holland, J. H. (1998). *Emergence: From chaos to order.* Oxford, UK, and New York: Oxford University Press.

Hoverstadt, P. (2008). *The fractal organization: Creating sustainable organizations with the viable systems model.* Chichester, UK: Wiley.

Hurst, D. K. (1995). *Crisis and renewal: Meeting the challenge of organizational change.* Boston: Harvard Business School Press.

Kaplan, R. S., & Norton, D. P. (1996). Using the balanced scorecard as a strategic management system. *Harvard Business Review, 74*(1), 75–85.

Kellerman, B. (2008). *Followership: How followers are creating change and changing leaders*. Boston: Harvard Business School Press.

Kelly, S., Iszatt White, M., Martin, D., & Rouncefield, M. (2006). Leadership refrains: Patterns of leadership. *Leadership, 2,* 181–201.

Levy, D. (1994). Chaos theory and strategy: Theory, application, and managerial implications. *Strategic Management Journal, 15,* 167–178.

Lewin, R., & Regine, B. (1999). *The soul at work: Unleashing the power of complexity science for business success*. London: Orion Business.

Logan, D., King, J., & Fischer-Wright, H. (2008). *Tribal leadership: Leveraging natural groups to build a thriving organization*. New York: Collins.

Malik, P. (2004). An introduction to fractal dynamics. *Journal of Human Values, 10,* 99–109.

Mandelbrot, B. B. (1982). *The fractal geometry of nature*. New York: WH Freeman.

Meyer, C., & Davis, S. (2003). *It's alive: The coming convergence of information, biology, and business*. New York: Texere.

Moore, G. A. (2006). *Dealing with Darwin: How great companies innovate at every phase of their evolution*. Chichester, UK: Capstone.

Morgan, G. (2006). *Images of organization* (4th ed.). Thousand Oaks, CA, and London: Sage.

Morrison, K. (2002). *School leadership and complexity theory*. London and New York: RoutledgeFalmer.

Olson, E. E., & Eoyang, G. H. (2001). *Facilitating organization change: Lessons from complexity science*. San Francisco: Jossey-Bass Pfeiffer.

Pascale, R. T. (1999). Surfing the edge of chaos. *Sloan Management Review, 40*(3), 83–94.

Pascale, R. T., Millemann, M., & Gioja, L. (2000). *Surfing the edge of chaos: The laws of nature and the new laws of business*. London and New York: Texere.

Poole, E. (2008). Baptizing management. *Studies in Christian Ethics, 21,* 85–97.

Raelin, J. A. (2003). *Creating leaderful organizations: How to bring out leadership in everyone*. San Francisco: Berret-Koehler.

Ritchie, R., & Deakin Crick, R. (2007). *Distributing leadership for personalizing learning*. London and New York: Network Continuum.

Simpson, P., & French, R. (2006). Negative capability and the capacity to think in the present moment: Some implications for leadership practice. *Leadership, 2,* 245–255.

Stacey, R. (1995). The science of complexity: An alternative perspective for strategic change processes. *Strategic Management Journal, 16,* 477–495.

Stacey, R. D., Griffin, D., & Shaw, P. (2000). *Complexity and management: Fad or radical challenge to systems thinking?* London and New York: Routledge.

Streatfield, P. J. (2001). *The paradox of control in organizations.* Abingdon, UK, and New York: Routledge.

Sweeney, K., & Griffiths, F. (Eds.). (2002). *Complexity and healthcare: An introduction.* Abingdon, UK: Radcliffe Medical Press.

Tourish, D., & Vatcha, N. (2005). Charismatic leadership and corporate cultism at Enron: The elimination of dissent, the promotion of conformity and organizational collapse. *Leadership, 1,* 455–480.

Wheatley, M. J. (1999). *Leadership and the new science: Discovering order in a chaotic world* (2nd ed.). San Francisco: Berrett-Koehler.

Wheatley, M. J. (2005). *Finding our way: Leadership for an uncertain time.* San Francisco: Berrett-Koehler.

Wheatley, M. J., & Kellner-Rogers, M. (1996). *A simpler way.* San Francisco: Berrett-Koehler.

Wineberg, R. (2005). *Fractal leadership: What if the way you think about your organisation is wrong?* Newstead, AUS: Smart Leadership.

YouTube. (2008). *Spontaneous order in people, markets, societies, and neurons.* Retrieved from www.youtube.com/watch?v=5w5aJvVCc0Q&feature =related.

Zimmerman, B., & Hurst, D. K. (1993). Breaking the boundaries: The fractal organization. *Journal of Management Inquiry, 2,* 334–355.

Transformation Through Artistry

Where No One Stays a Statue

Mark Nepo

It was a sunny day
and I went to the park
and sat on a bench. I was
one of many coming out
from under our rocks
to warm and lengthen.

He was two benches down,
a gentle older man
staring off into the place
between things, beyond
any simple past, staring
into the beginning or the end,
it was hard to say.

When he came up
our eyes met
and he knew I'd seen him
journey there and back.

There was no point in looking away.
And so, he shuffled over
and sat beside me. The sun
moved behind the one cloud
and he finally said
in half a quiver, "How
can we go there together?"

I searched my small mind
for an answer. At this,
he looked away and the sun came out
and I realized this is what the lonely
sages of China were talking about,
what the moon has whispered
before turning full for centuries,
what dancers leap for, what violinists
dream after fevering their last note.

But I was awkward and unsure.
He stared, as if to search my will,
and after several minutes,
he just patted my hand
and left.

I watched him
darken and brighten in the sun
and vowed to look
in the folds of every cry
for a way through
and hoped someday
to meet him there.

Improvising Transformation

Leadership Lessons from Improvisational Theater

James M. Mohr

Despite all of the leadership theory, dialogue about leadership, and new academic programs studying leadership, there simply exists no defined script for engaging in leadership in the real world in real time. Leaders are often called to make decisions in complex, ambiguous, and ever-evolving environments. These decisions can have lasting and possibly far-reaching effects. The difficulty in decision-making processes increases as leaders attempt to transform their organizations to adapt to new competitive pressures, changes in technology, and the continual flow of new information into the organizational system.

At times we may think our leaders are in control and that our organizations are following well-developed strategic change plans, but in reality our leaders are often making things up as they go along. In short, they are improvising. Leaders must engage in decision-making processes within quickly changing environments, and they may not always have the time to think about how to apply individual leadership theories to specific situations. It is in these situations, when they cannot ponder decisions for long periods of time, that their essence, core values, beliefs, and sense of the world come into play and help them make their decisions. In this chapter, I argue that improvisational theater can provide us with a deeper understanding of how we can tap into our creative, emotional, intellectual, physical, and spiritual cores to become better decision makers and more successful leaders during times of transformation. For it is in this ability to improvise that we can either achieve success and greatness or meet with failure and stagnation.

Improvising Organizations

The traditional assumptions about organizations and their environments are that they are knowable, predictable, and controllable (Crossan, Lane, White, & Klus, 1996). These assumptions lead to attempts to manage transformation and change through prescribed practices such as vision statements, strategic plans, goal setting, and other conventional tools. However, even when we employ the best of these tools, change efforts often fail. This failure has led researchers to explore improvisation as a method of understanding organizations and explaining change.

Improvisational theater is a disciplined theatrical process in which the players co-create stories on the spot, often based on suggestions they get from the audience. Simply put, there is no script and the players make everything up as they go. It is this process of "making stuff up" that encouraged Weick (1993) to propose theatrical improvisation as a new metaphor for organizational change, because change is often emergent, can come from any source, and is an ongoing process. Since Weick's initial writing, improvisational theater has been incorporated into ideas and models about organizational learning (Dyba, 2000; Yanow, 2001), managerial techniques (Crossan et al., 1996), organizational transformation (Orlikowski, 1996), and strategy development (Kantor, 2002). Improvisational theater as a metaphor has been able to provide many valuable insights into these different areas for organizational transformation and change. In this chapter, I extend the metaphor of improvisational theater to the process of leadership and examine the lessons we can garner from this theater practice to transform not just our understanding of organizational change but how we act and react as leaders.

Improvisation and Leadership

One thing that seems to surprise people is that improvisational theater has an underlying structure that helps the players to be connected to one another. One of the major differences between the structure of improvisation and that of business is that for improvisation the structure is considered a jumping-off point for exploring possibilities rather than as rigidly defined boundaries for limiting action. The foundation of this structure is built around two simple sounding phrases: "Yes and" and "Make your partner look good." These phrases make it possible for improvisers to co-create stories together, secure in the knowledge that all of the players are taking the same journey in making something new and that they can rely on each other for support. Both phrases and the sense of security they engender in the players encourages them to take action.

The "Yes and" principle engages everyone in a collaborative action in which everyone recognizes what was said, affirms it, and then extends it so that the possibilities within an idea can be explored. The principle "Make your partner look good" means that you focus on your partner rather than yourself and you take responsibility for both of you (Koppett, 2001). Both of these principles focus the individual on the other; this type of focus is an essential component to the co-creation process.

These two phrases allow for everyone in the organization to trust others and to believe that they can co-create something in the moment, change direction, and rethink previously made decisions. It now becomes possible to reach into the irrational component of the change process. Though we may expect our leadership and organizations to be rational, we know that rationality is more of an ideal than truth. Change often gets stuck because the attempts to manage it did not consider anything outside of the expected and predicted.

Hatch, Kostera, and Kozminski (2005, p. 9) commented that aesthetics enables leaders "to address and inspire people in ways that lie beyond rationality—emotion, creativity, and ethics." Improvisational theater helps us develop this ability to go beyond the rational everyday and tap into our intuition and core self as a key leadership practice. My personal experiences with improvisation have changed my thinking about leadership. I now think of leadership as a creative and imaginative process realized through community commitment and action rooted in six key principles of being. The principles are (1) trust, (2) presence, (3) dialogical process, (4) emergence, (5) co-creativity, and (6) openness. My understanding of these principles is that they are not tools to be pulled out of a leader's tool belt at exactly the right moment; rather, these principles are about a way of being in the world. They are a reflection of how a leader sees, acts, and reacts to life at all times, and they can be developed.

Richards (1995, p. 36) commented, "All work can be artful, but the artfulness lies on our approach to the work and not in the work itself." It seems to me that the word *leadership* could easily replace the word *work* in Richards's quote. Leadership is an artful process, and exactly what that process looks like is determined by the attitude and approach of the leader. The leader's core being is what determines how he or she interacts with others and the world. When I talk about a way of being in the world, I speak of the manner in which the leader exists and the worldview from which he or she approaches life and its challenges.

The improvisational principles are not intellectual exercises but reflect genuine and deeply felt beliefs that guide the leader through the process of change. These principles do not exist in a hierarchical form and are not mutually exclusive; some ideas in one principle overlap with the others. Rather than thinking of the principles in a linear form, I have come to think of them in terms of a collage. As a collage, the principles have deep connections that interact and impact one another rather than being discrete entities that are to be mastered individually.

The collage image is used because it is a form of artistic expression in which diverse elements are juxtaposed in unexpected ways. These diverse elements are not placed within discrete boundaries; rather, they overlap one another, build up and under each other, and come to have a new life and meaning beyond their original intent. In fact, the collage often disrupts the meanings we have placed on the objects in the collage and forces us to rethink what we believe we know and to reconsider our actions. The collage collapses our preconceived notions and opens us up to nonlinear approaches to thinking about our core selves, leadership, and our relationships with others.

The Six Principles

Trust is the first principle of improvisational leadership and the essential component of making it work. There are four components to trust: trust in yourself, trust in your team, your team's trust in you, and trust in the process. Without these four forms of trust, leading in this manner is difficult if not impossible. Yukl (1998) explained that the leader's ability to develop trust was an essential component of building a follower's commitment to a vision. In fact, more than four decades of research have demonstrated the significance of trust in leadership, with trust being positively associated with work outcomes, work attitudes, citizenship behaviors, and job performance (Dirks & Ferrin, 2002).

The second principle is being *present* to what is happening. Being present means one is mindful of one's self, others, the environment, the relationships between these three areas, and the patterns that develop in, through, and because of these relationships. The improvisers must be completely aware not only of what fellow performers are doing and saying on stage but also completely aware of the environment and of what the individual performer is saying and doing (Halpern & Close, 1994). Likewise, a leader must be completely present in the moment when listening to others, giving direction, or observing the environment in which she finds her business. Nakai and Schultz (2000) explained that mindfulness can help a leader be more flexible, resilient, and adept at working in complex and changeable environments. It permits openness to new information, awareness of multiple perspectives, and attention to today's challenges.

Through a mindful disposition, the leader can relate better to others in the organization and is able to see patterns as they develop. Recognizing patterns allows the leader to develop a deeper level of understanding of reality (Anderson & Johnson, 1997). Maintaining an improvisational approach to life allows for the development of one's pattern recognition ability. By seeing the patterns that develop in a scene, the improviser is able to create a better and more meaningful scene (Halpern & Close, 1994). Likewise, the leader who finds patterns of behavior and events is better able to see how different problems are interconnected, allowing the leader to implement better and more comprehensive solutions than would be possible if he or she were blind to these patterns (Haines, 1998).

The third principle is engaging in a *dialogic process*. There is an improvisation game called One-Word Story. In this game the players are lined up on stage and then, through each one saying one word, they form sentences and then a story; listening is essential, as it is impossible to predict what the other person will say (Halpern & Close, 1994). Together, the players are creating something new that previously did not exist. They are working collaboratively and no one is trying to win, as the game's point is to allow a new creation (the story) to emerge from their collaborative effort.

Bohm (2004) explained that dialogue is not a win-lose proposition. In dialogue, each person is working with the others to generate new knowledge, to uncover something previously unknown or unnoticed. Dialogue is not something that can be forced, but leaders can create an environment in which dialogue is encouraged to emerge naturally from the relationships among the people in the organization. A leader with an improvisational attitude is able to provide a safe space for the emergence of dialogue. Such a leader recognizes the importance of confirming every person in his organization. Through confirmation, a leader recognizes the humanity of the other and accepts the other as important, relevant, and fully human (Laing, 1994). This type of confirming process is an essential component to the improviser.

An integral part of being a successful improviser is to be comfortable with the development of novel ideas and allowing a story to emerge out of what may seem like chaos. A belief in the *emergent* nature of things is the fourth principle of being a leader can use as guidance. According to Axelrod and Cohen, emergent properties are "properties of the system that the separate parts do not have" (2000, p. 15). It is through the interaction and relationships of the people in the organization with each other and with their environment that permit novel ideas to form and be implemented. When a leader is guided by the emergent principle, he or she recognizes the need for the free flow and development of these relationships to continue the growth of the organization.

Halpern and Close commented, "An actor following each moment through to the next is constantly making discoveries" (1994, p. 71). All actors in an improvised performance are discovering new things about their characters and environment through their interactions with others. The actors allow these new discoveries to emerge from the interactions without attempting to block them. They are open to going in new directions based on what their fellow performers are saying and doing. A leader guided by the emergent principle understands that he or she is not the principle source of ideas, action, or direction. This type of leader provides opportunities for meaningful interactions among his or her followers because the leader understands that the best new ideas will come through these interactions. The followers are given the freedom to create new ideas and to bring these ideas forward without fear of ridicule. This principle of a belief in the emergent nature of things does not mean that all of the ideas generated through an improvisational manner are accepted; only that the ideas will be respected and given full and genuine consideration. It is not possible for all ideas to be accepted, but it is possible to provide opportunities for the generation of multiple ideas.

The fifth principle of being is the notion that the leader and followers *co-create* their organization, community, and world. Wheatley (1999) explained that we live in a participative universe and that through our relationships we co-create our world. When leaders and followers create an environment that is open to multiple perspectives and ideas, they realize they cannot simply break down their process into discrete parts to analyze exactly what worked and did not work. Improvisers have often learned that after an amazing performance, they cannot break down the performance to discover what made it amazing. They learn to accept that it was the group process—performers trusting themselves and one another and honoring their connections—that created their success (Halpern & Close, 1994). The improvisational attitude is rooted in the belief that it takes everyone to co-create excellence. A leader who adapts this way of being will find that he or she is leading an organization in which everyone involved with it takes ownership for his or her actions, interactions, and for the organization.

Openness is the final principle for the improvisational leader. Openness is demonstrated through creating an environment in which risk taking and creativity are valued and encouraged. To create such an environment, people must feel that it is acceptable to fail and to learn from that failure. If failure is never an option, then risk taking and creativity become less possible. It is impossible to predict the outcome of a new strategy or plan, but it is possible to allow for the freedom for people to put forward outrageous, bizarre, and innovative ideas to be explored, examined, and even implemented. The improviser knows that he or she can take a leap of faith and try something risky in a scene, and that all of the other performers on the stage will catch him or her. There are no mistakes in improvisation, and when performers trust one another, they can take huge risks that may bring correspondingly huge rewards, especially when that risk is supported by the other performers.

Developing Improvisational Leaders

Improvisational leaders can help facilitate successful transformative processes not only because they can be adaptable but because they can create environments in which everyone feels they are part of the process and can be flexible to meet new demands. By building creative organizations where ideas, information, and energy flow through the entire entity, improvisational leaders create a structure that naturally withstands internal and external pressures that may threaten other organizations. There are four strategies that leaders can use to encourage and nurture improvisational leadership.

First, organizations need to *create shared spaces of creativity and openness* where everyone is invited to spark the fires of their imaginations to explore organizational successes and challenges to see what emerges from this collaborative exploration. These are spaces where risks are not only nurtured but demanded.

Second, leaders need to *respect everyone for his or her knowledge and experiences.* At times leaders must have a willingness to suspend what they think they know and listen to the perspectives and understandings of others. The knowledge, skills, and thoughts of all members need to rise into a conscious awareness to be shared with the leaders and other organizational members. However, leaders should not hide their own knowledge during this process of sharing; rather, they need to bring themselves fully into the discussions but not in a manner that shuts everyone down. A leader is one among equals who allows personal knowledge and experiences to flow into the awareness of others; together, then, everyone interacts with this information to create something new.

Third, leaders need to *recognize and reward people for teamwork and for being supportive of one another.* At times, the support person may be just as important as the person who is the "face" of a project, organization, or idea. By validating the supportive role, it becomes less necessary to be the person out in front and more important for everyone to work together to move a project forward.

Fourth, organizations need to *embrace inclusive practices* that allow for a diverse workforce to feel welcomed and wanted. These inclusive practices allow for people to be more focused on organizational success than spending their energy fighting a rigid system that is more concerned with compliance to arbitrary rules than supporting its employees.

Conclusion

In this chapter, I examined the structure of improvisational theater to determine leadership lessons that can guide leaders through the process of organizational transformation. The principles that have been discussed are meant to provide a structure that allows leaders to explore possibilities and not to limit action, just as the structure of improvisation does. These principles were explained to exist as the collage art form in which they can be joined in infinite combinations, creating infinite possibilities of infinite forms of expression of our leadership. They are not predefined barriers to limit movement, thought, or engagement with the world; rather, the principles help us to uncover the potential in every situation.

With the continual pressures for change being felt by organizations, leaders need to shift how they think of their leadership strategies. The world and our organizations no longer need the tyrant issuing orders from on high to the little people who must scurry and make those orders happen. No one person can have all of the knowledge, skills, and ideas to handle the continual flow of information, technological innovation, and cultural transformations that are happening. Leadership during chaotic times takes a person who can build trust, be present in the moment, engage in dialogic practice, respect the emergent nature of things, encourage a co-creative process, and be open to the possibilities. In essence, the new leaders need to be improvisers who can see past the rational and tap into the creative source of everyone within the organization.

References

Anderson, V., & Johnson, L. (1997). *Systems thinking basics: From concepts to causal loops.* Waltham, MA: Pegasus.

Axelrod, R., & Cohen, M. D. (2000). *Harnessing complexity: Organizational implications of a scientific frontier.* New York: Basic Books.

Bohm, D. (2004). *On dialogue.* London: Routledge Classics.

Crossan, M. M., Lane, H. W., White, R. E., & Klus, L. (1996). The improvising organization: Where planning meets opportunity. *Organizational Dynamics, 24*(4), 20–35.

Dirks, K. T., & Ferrin, D. L. (2002). Trust in leadership: Meta-analytic findings and implications for research and practice. *Journal of Applied Psychology, 87*(4), 611–628.

Dyba, T. (2000). Improvisation in small software organizations. *IEEE Software, 17*(5), 82–87.

Haines, S. G. (1998). *The manager's pocket guide to system's thinking and learning.* Amherst, MA: HRD Press.

Halpern, C., & Close, D. (1994). *Truth in comedy.* Colorado Springs: Meriwether.

Hatch, M. J., Kostera, M., & Kozminski, A. (2005). *The three faces of leadership: Manager, artist, priest.* Malden, MA: Blackwell.

Kantor, R. M. (2002). Strategy as improvisational theater. *MIT Sloan Management Review, 43*(2), 76–81.

Koppett, K. (2001). *Training to imagine.* Sterling, VA: Stylus.

Laing, R. D. (1994). Confirmation and disconfirmation. In R. Anderson, K. N. Cissna, & R. C. Arnett (Eds.), *The reach of dialogue: Confirmation, voice, and community* (pp. 73–78). Cresskill, NJ: Hampton Press.

Nakai, P., & Schultz, R. (2000). *The mindful corporation: Liberating the human spirit at work.* New York: Leadership Press.

Orlikowski, W. J. (1996). Improvising organizational transformation over time: A situated change perspective. *Information Systems Research, 7*(1), 63–92.

Richards, D. (1995). *Artful work: Awakening joy, meaning, and commitment in the workplace.* San Francisco: Berrett-Koehler.

Weick, K. E. (1993). Organizational redesign as improvisation. In G. P. Huber & W. H. Glick (Eds.), *Organizational change and redesign: Ideas and insights for improving performance* (pp. 346–379). New York: Oxford University Press.

Wheatley, M. J. (1999). *Leadership and the new science: Discovering order in a chaotic world* (2nd ed.). San Francisco: Berrett-Koehler.

Yanow, D. (2001). Learning in and from improvising: Lessons from theater for organizational learning. *Reflections, 2*(4), 58–65.

Yukl, G. (1998). *Leadership in organization.* Englewood Cliffs, NJ: Prentice-Hall.

Transforming Leadership through the Power of the Imagination

Michael Jones

"My Business is Circumference," poet Emily Dickinson writes (Linscott, 1959, p. 25, from a letter written to Alfred Higginson dated July 2, 1862). This is also the business of leadership. To understand the significance of circumference, we need to acknowledge the new mind-set required of leaders for integrative whole mind learning. As we struggle with new discontinuities, fragmentation, and sudden change, it is vital for leaders to think in more complex and holistic ways. This thinking involves a shift in focus from a narrow and reductive emphasis on individualism based upon an industrial model of managing, in which the leader is the strong, dependable, self-made individual or hero, toward a style of leading that expands the circumference within which the leader leads.

In the future, leaders will not be remembered for their professional, technical, or cost-cutting skills but for their wisdom, empathy, presence, intuition, and artistry. It will be a way of leading that is more relational focused and based upon creating an empathic resonance with others as a networker, connector, and convener of webs and communities. We could imagine this new relationship to be like the musician's open stage, where individuals with diverse voices come together in an ever-widening circumference of collective engagement and where—even when they are "strangers" to one another—they create beautiful musical collaborations together.

Leaders engaging in the shift of mind from being heroes to artists need to cultivate new disciplines for accessing the subtle power of the imagination. The new engagement involves understanding that while strategy and tactics may help leaders be effective technicians, in order to be good artists they need also to listen deeply and get a feeling for things—in other words to be attuned to the unheard melody that is emerging in the space between the notes. Emily Dickinson (Todd, 1896, p. 139) brings to light this unheard melody—of the sense of being touched from another place—when she writes:

> This world is not conclusion;
> —A sequel stands beyond,
> Invisible, as music,
> —But positive, as sound.

Listening for the Unheard Melody

Dickinson's words bring to mind a line from another poem, one that describes "the beast of sound caged within the music bars." These words offer a contrasting world in which what speaks to us from that other place is not wild and free but contained and caged behind the bars. It is a world where, if we are to maintain order and predictability, the wild and unruly elements—the beasts—of the imagination must be constrained. Too often we assume a Faustian bargain—one in which we willingly trade off the promise of a sequel, of something greater and more beautiful just beyond—for the assurance of certainty, clarity, and predictability in the moment.

Yet most, if only at a young age, have experienced the power of the imagination—we have tasted the sweet elixir of being set free and unconstrained—riding on the fresh wind, the doorway flying open wide and . . . "Life rushing in." As a friend said to me after reading the lines of the poem about the beast being caged behind the music bars, "You don't cage the animals do you? You dance with them!"

It is true, additionally, that as a pianist the melody I listened for was not only in the notes but also in the pauses, the tone, the rhythm, the feeling, and the sensitivity of touch—the dance that lay in the spaces between. In order to be attuned to the deeper music, to let go and let be, I learned to listen and be open and responsive to whatever was coming next, to be alive to the moment and to every possibility. The surroundings, the listeners, sense impressions: everything that danced along the periphery of my attention became a part of the melody and inspiration I heard in my mind and heart.

There is so much that inspires the free flow of the music beyond the physical notes, a stream of conscious and emergent creation that cannot always be anticipated or planned in advance. This is the artist's work, to make the invisible visible through being alive to their own felt experience including all that they have seen and been nourished by. With this aliveness they can be responsive to what the moment calls for. In a time of rapid and unexpected change when so little can be understood or controlled in advance, this is the work of leadership as well.

The Leader as Artist

The shift, therefore, from the leader as hero to the leader as artist involves a transformation in awareness from performance to presence, from the visible to the invisible, from answers to questions, from lines to circles, from uniformity to uniqueness, from abstraction to beauty, from efficiency to improvisation, and from a focus on language that is instrumental for achieving certain goals and outcomes to the expressive power of stories and the authenticity of one's own personal voice. These are disciplines that awaken the power of the imagination. They help transform our mechanistic or industrial view of our world to one that is more subtle and sustainable—a transcendent vision that is more creative, organic, and whole. Mastering these disciplines is how an artistic viewpoint can be helpful to business leaders. As practices of the imagination, they enable leaders to accept their own vulnerability and not knowing—of living into the deeper questions and embracing a world of uncertainty with a much greater unknown. Even as we sense the possibility this transformation holds for us, why is it so difficult for us to engage this awareness most of the time?

In part, this resistance comes because we are the inheritors of a story that is our legacy from Industrial Age myths. In this story, we often experience our own spontaneity and creativity caged behind the music bars. It is as if from the moment we stepped onto the schoolyard we also stepped into our own mechanistic cage. Being in this cage educates us to a very specific and particular reality, one so sharply illuminated that it is difficult, even impossible, to see beyond this story we have been given and believe there is something more.

My own spontaneity and creativity became apparent to me some years ago when my partner Judy and I decided to sell our Toronto home and travel for six months or so. While we trusted our decision, we struggled with how to proceed. So we planned our route and called ahead to friends and left voice-mails to let them know we were coming and might stay for a while. They didn't call back! A colleague, sensing our difficulties, said, "This is a unique opportunity—a time to travel with the light of a candle rather than a flashlight." These simple words changed everything, not only for how we traveled, but also for how to live and how to lead in uncertain times. Stepping out of our life as we had known it helped us see more clearly the cage we were in.

The Myths We Live By

The cage I am referring to is an old story—one composed of a set of myths that, like the imperviousness of steel bars—inhibit the free flow of imaginative experience. The myths have been inherited from the legacy of our industrial past; because we are still being educated for the Industrial Age, these myths are still very much with us—in our work, our families, our communities and organizations, and our way of being. Like the fish swimming in the sea, myths often absorb many of our assumptions regarding how to think, act, and feel that we don't know that they are there. The myths contribute to a worldview, however, based upon false certainties, excessive control, limited possibility, and imagined fears—fears that are reinforced through the telling and retelling of a story that we have been conditioned to believe is true.

These myths include . . .

Perfection and the Myth of the Absolute Truth

With this myth we give up our inner knowing in deference to the credentials or experience of an external authority. We are given to believe that there is a right answer to everything, and for others to be right, we must be wrong. Behind this belief is the prevailing fear that if others don't conform to our view, chaos will ensue. When we accept this myth as true, we give over control to experts and specialists, to policies, outside authorities, and standards that we believe have perfected this truth to which we try to subscribe. This flashlight world pushes us toward the hunt for one all-encompassing perfect Truth with a large T. The assumption that this truth exists, and our search for it, blinds us to the subtlety and presence of the truth of our gifts and sense of self. This latter is the truth with a small t. By serving as stewards to our own innate potential, even if it is through increments both imperfect and incomplete, we also shift the focus of attention from authority to authenticity; in so doing, we learn to lead from our gifts and inner wisdom rather than from external edicts and what an expert said. Ultimately, what reinforces this myth is the fear of risking being wrong, of our own sense of inadequacy, and that our own uniqueness will, in some fundamental way, not be accepted by others.

Isolation and the Myth of Separation

This search for the absolute truth compresses our world into what is immediately before us and near at hand. We have no patience for ambiguity and uncertainties—and this separation often leads to the neglect of the "other" or anything that is not in direct relationship to the absolute truth we seek. In this myth we objectify our world, negate the other, and force movement toward a predetermined goal or end state. We also risk seeing those who disagree with us as being "not like us"—and therefore also being not fully human. This negation of the other forms the basis for creating insiders and outsiders, of clans and tribes whose differences become insurmountable. This inwardness leads, in turn, to a sense of disconnection from the whole, from a sense of beauty, of belonging and connection to place. In place of embracing the wholeness of life, we become addicted to the celebration of busyness, to a sense of personal entitlement, a turning away from the stewardship of the commons and public good and a preoccupation with our private life. The myth of separation is based upon the fear of being excluded and an apprehension that disconnects us from the source of our own inspiration, sense of belonging, and connection to home and to who we naturally are.

Control and the Myth of Efficiency

With the myth of efficiency we believe that everything is up to us. This myth implies that it is possible, even preferable, to bring all of life's unruly elements under our direct control. The belief underlying a notion of efficiency is that we fear that if we don't use planning, logic, control, and strategy to force and hold things together, everything will spin out of control. When we give up our trust or relationship in the other, then it becomes a self-fulfilling prophecy: whatever grace and cooperation may be available to us is overshadowed by our need for dominance through planning, measurement, analysis, and/or control.

Limits and the Myth of Scarcity

With the myth of scarcity we assume there is not enough to go around. We assume that creative ability and original thought are thinly distributed and, therefore, for one person to succeed, one or more must lose. With this myth we live in a capricious and unpredictable universe. Life itself becomes a zero-sum game in which limits abound and there will never be enough to go around. Under these conditions, the whole must give way to the interests of the parts. The fear of not having enough distorts the deeper truth that while we must work within certain limits of balance—when we act in a spirit of abundance and generosity—the universe is replenished, not diminished, by the creative demands we place upon it.

Changing the Light We Lead By

I would love to live like water
Instead of initiating movement
I want to be movement
in a continuous unfolding process
of becoming and dissolving
into something else.

—*Michael Jones*

At the present time we are between stories—too often we lead by rote, by script, by credentials, by strategy or tactics, by our five-year plan, or by what the expert says. We subscribe to the flashlight world and make absolute its qualities of purpose, direction, focus, willfulness, action, and clear sightedness. We miss how, as these qualities fall out of balance, they become absolutes. These qualities reinforce the myths of perfection, absolute truth, separation, efficiency, scarcity, and control. We hunger for what the candlelight brings—for landscape, music, art, subtlety, nuance, and the gifts they bring of ambiguity, trust, silence, courage, surrender, willingness, connection, and risk.

The leader, subsequently, needs to balance not one but two bottom lines. The first is strategic, focused on assessing, prioritizing, and reporting. Most leaders must learn to succeed in an outcome-oriented, mission-based, and document-driven world. A second bottom line is one that speaks to our own longing and to the timeless needs and wisdom of the heart—what we may think of as, in the words of psychotherapist Carla M. Dahl, "leadership by unfolding" "When I am tempted to lead by role, by technique or worse, someone else's compass, John O'Donohue's poem 'Fluent' reminds me of the way the river has to trust its own unfolding. No leader can see the end from the beginning, no matter how strategic the plan" (Dahl, quoted in Intrator & Scribner, 2007, p. 82). The leader's work is somehow to find balance between the intellect's passion for strategy, action, and outcome with the heart and the imagination's affinity for the unknown. These myths are a natural result of an overemphasis on cultivating the strategic mind without at the same time cultivating the intelligence of an empathic and imaginative heart.

Finding Meaning in a New Story

In speaking of this world out of balance, author Joseph Chilton Pierce (1992) offers this caution: "Should the intellect win the battle with the heart's intelligence then the war will be lost for all of us. . . . We will be just an experiment that failed" (p. xx). In other words, we cannot rely upon the intellect's understanding to find our way to the other side of a world that is of its own invention; nor can we apply the same strategies to change our world that we used to create it. For this experiment to succeed we will need to be guided by a fresh set of images and questions, ones that connect us to the roots of our own aliveness and creative imagination. For example, the myth of perfection invites the deeper question, Who am I really? The myth of separation, Where is home? The myth of efficiency, How do I let go and let be? And the myth of scarcity, What is enough? These are candle-light questions—the answers are not immediate but instead awaken the heart to new possibilities and encourage us to reflect and connect more deeply with our own unfolding nature.

As we reflect upon the candlelight questions, new and more opaque figures, images that are often impossible to see in a flashlight world, begin to emerge from the shadows. These are the "powerful strangers" that were lost to us when we began to hold the imagination suspect—caged the beast—and systematically disenchanted our world. As they come into full presence, they may serve as wise guides to help make visible a hidden world of interconnection and wholeness—a complex mythic world rich with archetypal symbols and imagery that liberate the imagination and awaken the heart.

The Steward: Finding Inspiration in Our Own Life

> For as long as the gift is used people will live.
> —Black Elk

Behind the myth of absolute truth, for example, is an archetypal image, the Steward. The Steward provides the connective tissue that brings us together. It connects us to the sense of our own truth, integrity, wisdom, and intuition. The image of the Steward holds the space of possibility for our gifts and talents and the courage to be true to one's own calling. Being open to possibility includes accepting the gifts of our true identity and insight and finding faith and inspiration—the music—in one's own life. The Steward takes a stand in service of our own inner truth and for the gift and uniqueness we hold for ourselves and others. With the Steward, we find the wisdom, inspiration, and courage to let go of ideological truths in favor of our own embodied truth and inner knowing. This archetype of the Steward establishes, protects, and holds the integrity of boundaries of the whole. It tends the rich soil to keep our vision and dreams rooted in a sense of and significance of place. It aligns us with our own inner nature and true path to leadership and helps us act with coherence and integrity in service of our deepest work in the world.

The Enchanter: Discovering Our Own Way of Seeing

> My dad could name one hundred miles of coastline
> by the taste of the air.
>
> —Annie Proulx

Behind the myth of separation is the archetypal image of the Enchanter. The Enchanter helps us discern the almost imperceptible distinctions and nuances between occurrences. It connects us to the transcendent. It is the gentle defender of beauty. Beauty helps us see—it offers us the gifts of perception and adaptivity so that we may make finely tuned adjustments in the moment. The Enchanter also helps establish an empathic connection to our world. It connects us to place, to nature and to inner stillness, to patience and to receptivity for "otherness" as embodied in the company of strangers and new experiences. In a time of dislocation, the Enchanter instills a sense of hope, belonging, and inspiration. By acknowledging the centrality of Eros, the sensual and the aesthetic, the Enchanter also brings into being a sense of balance and wholeness to protect us from the isolation that an adherence to an absolute truth often imposes upon us.

The Weaver: Discovering What Our Life Is Trying to Be

> There's a thread you follow. It goes among
> things that change.
>
> —William Stafford, The Way It Is (1998, p. 42)

Behind the myth of efficiency is the Weaver. The Weaver draws the threads together and weaves magical fabrics of shared meaning and emergent possibility. It sees the world from many different angles and invites new possibilities in a spirit of generosity, detachment, perspective, and novelty. In this manner, the Weaver dances along the boundaries and in so doing perceives webs of connection across different worlds and perceived difference and does so with infinite mastery, ease, and grace. Just as musicians know that when they are playing, they are also being played, the Weaver holds and accepts the many alternative definitions of what is true. Through an expanded awareness and discernment, the Weaver helps us recognize that we cannot control everything—that our hyper-efficiency and excessive control will inevitably lead to unintended consequences. By suspending our certainties and accepting the ambiguous nature of our world, we are available for surprise and the natural emergence of unforeseen opportunities.

The Visionary: Finding Authority in Our Own Subjective Experience

> The limits of my language mean the limits of my world.
>
> —*Ludwig Wittgenstein*

The fear of scarcity conceals the archetype of the Visionary. The Visionary is the teacher and purveyor of language who transforms our reality through the power of story and voice. The Visionary does not just speak but is brought to speech through allowing what is most deeply personal to speak through itself. In allowing the "speaking through," the Visionary sees vision not as an ultimate goal or end state but as a powerful instrument for the articulation of our deepest vocation, which carries the same root as *voice*. In allowing the "speaking through," the Visionary gives meaning to our dreams and possibilities and offers hope and perspective where everyone else sees despair. This sense of vocation and embodiment of the Word is the aspect of the imagination that most embodies the energy of language not only to inform but also to transform and therefore serve as the source of abundance, of blessing, wholeness, affirmation, order, integration, and new life. The Visionary is the voice of recognition and aspiration. It sees and calls out the gift of abundance in the other; and, in doing so, the Visionary sees and articulates the shared intention, aspirations, and common voice of the whole.

Awakening the Commons of the Imagination

> When we discover what leads to us feeling more
> alive, we will have found the key to bringing the
> commons to life.
> —*Michael Jones (2006, p. 169)*

Together, the presence of these archetypes, by whatever name we give them, helps to awaken a commons of the imagination. As we free these deep archetypal figures from their cages, the energy they release opens doorways to new patterns and pathways to leadership—pathways that, while they may be understood through the intellect, can only be manifest through experience. Together, these pathways offer new and imaginative forms and ways of acting and being, reminding us that we cannot always force the river, that our strength is also found in waiting, sensing, and listening in order to hear how the river speaks to us. Working with both subtle and strong forces of leading from behind and being attuned to the nature of time's natural unfolding, we begin to unfold the true vocation of the artist-leader.

While awakening the commons is the work of now, it is also the work of a lifetime. It is in the nature of the imagination that in one moment there is nothing and then there is something. We can make explicit everything in the creative process but this; yet it seems that it is this—the mystery in how and when the power of archetypal energies make their appearance—that makes the difference between actions that truly interconnect and move us forward and actions that don't. Being aware of these archetypal energies suggests that at some very early and critical stage in the creative process there is a need to release and let go of oneself. Like the artist, the creative process involves a willingness and trust to lead—and also to be led, opening the door for the insights of these subtle forces to come in. In other words, they are paradoxical in that these subtle forces are both very powerful and also very shy. If we bring too much of the critical attention of the strategic mind in search of their tangible presence, the subtle forces are no longer there; consequently, shining the flashlight in search of concrete evidence of the existence of these imaginative forces may actually cause the very thing we are looking for to retreat and hide.

When these ancient and timeless archetypes are awakened in us, however, we can see beyond our experience of fear and limitation. Through their collective eyes and ears we can see and engage a world of infinite complexity. In the presence of the archetypes, we may also restore to the world of myth its true purpose, which is not to promote false truths or limit our actions through fear and isolation, but instead to reenchant our world with the experiencing of wonder, awe, and possibility. Most important, it becomes possible to communicate intangible realities that cannot be passed along in any other way.

In conclusion, to transform our leadership we need to respect and understand the nature of the gift in art and learn to be good stewards of the soil of the commons so that our true potential as leaders may take seed and grow. In the past, most every community had a commons—a community "front porch or village green" that was available for everyone's use, not only for crops and livestock but for art and music and for the communities' story to be reimagined and retold. For many, the absence of the commons has been a source of indefinable but palpable unrest. It is like a hunger for which we can find no cause or cure.

We are very practiced at setting goals, defining outcomes, and managing our time, but less so in creating fertile ground for balancing action with gestation—with time for seeding, rest, reflection, absorption, walking, dreaming, questioning, noticing, practicing, and being. This was the gift of the commons' space. Nothing was laid down in any predictable pattern or routine.

Rather it was a space between—an "allowing space"—to which each was welcomed, friend and stranger alike, not necessary to do but to be with whatever evolved in the form of ideas, stories, images, and emergent meanings. In his book *The Way It Is*, William Stafford writes in the poem "A Ritual to Read to Each Other,"

> *And so I appeal to a voice, to something shadowy,*
> *a remote important region in all who talk:*
> *though we could fool each other, we should consider—*
> *lest the parade of our mutual life get lost in the dark.*
>
> *For it is important that awake people be awake,*
> *or a breaking line may discourage them back to sleep;*
> *the signals we give—yes or no, or maybe—*
> *should be clear: the darkness around us is deep.*
>
> —William Stafford (1998, p. 75)

Stafford's words remind us that for years our world was illuminated not by the flashlight but by the opaque shadows and crackling light of the fire—our circumference enlarged not through our roles as managers, executives, employees, or consultants but through our presence as storytellers, teachers, warriors, stewards, poets, musicians, enchanters, and weavers. Through the language of music, story, poetry, myth, prophecy, and song we appealed to a voice to light our way in the darkness. As we awaken the power of the imagination, we may turn again to those same timeless voices in the shadows from our past and—by uniting together modern thought with ancient wisdom—make a new appeal.

Acknowledgment

This article was originally published in the *Integral Leadership Review*, Volume IX, No. 2—March 2009.

References

Intrator, S., & Scribner, M. (2007). *Leading from within: Poetry that sustains the courage to lead*. San Francisco: Jossey-Bass.

Jones, M. (2006). *Artful leadership, awakening the commons of the imagination*. Bloomington, IN: Trafford.

Pierce, J. C. (1992). *Evolution's end: Claiming the potential of our intelligence*. New York: Harper Collins.

Stafford, W. (1998). *The way it is: New and selected poems*. St Paul: Graywolf.

Todd, M. L. (Ed.) (1896). *Poems by Emily Dickinson*. Boston: Roberts Brothers.

Leadership

A Journey of Transformation

Rick Warm

Leadership is not generally looked upon as a journey; yet leadership can be a developmental process that is clearly a transformational journey—a journey that has the potential to transform both the leader and ultimately those led. During the second half of the twentieth century, a young scholar began his own journey through the dusty annals of ancient world myths. Joseph Campbell became possibly the world's best-known comparative mythologist, drawing a unique understanding of the journey of transformation, which he called the *hero's journey*, from hundreds of myths of diverse times and peoples across the world (Campbell, 1968). The heroic journey, what Campbell called the *monomyth*, takes place in the mythic realm and is about our inner quest for development, an attempt to understand our place in the world. It is about meaning and transcendence. "The passage of the mythological hero may be overground, incidentally; fundamentally it is inward—into depths where obscure resistances are overcome, and long lost, forgotten powers are revivified, to be made available for the transfiguration of the world" (p. 29).

Why is the hero's journey important to leadership? Campbell talks at great length of the journey as a path toward finding one's humanity. Myths, he explains, tell us of our humanity—how to be human. Parker Palmer, among others, has called the heroic journey an *inner journey*. "Go far enough on the inner journey, they all tell us—go past the ego toward true self—and you end up not lost in narcissism but returning to the world, bearing more gracefully the responsibilities that come with being human" (Palmer, 2000, p. 73). In this chapter, I explore the connection between the development of leaders and the hero's journey. I argue that leadership requires personal transformation that will ultimately allow the leader to help transform others.

Mythology and Leadership

The challenge we face in understanding mythology today is that though the motifs are the same, the cultures that they come from have changed. The search is on for a modern mythology we can all embrace. "We need myths that will identify the individual not with his local group but with the planet" (Campbell, 1988, p. 30). The contemporary struggle is to read the stories built on generations of wisdom, understand those motifs in a modern context, and allow them to develop naturally as they have for previous generations and eons. The challenge is remarkably similar to Gardner and Laskin's thoughts on visionary leadership. "The formidable challenge confronting the visionary leader is to offer a story, and an embodiment, that builds on the most credible of past syntheses, revisits them in the light of present concerns, leaves open a place for future events, and allows individual contributions by the persons in the group" (1995, p. 56).

Rost argues that the concept of leadership has become popular because it has "taken on mythological significance" (1991, p. 7). Clearly a fan of Campbell, Rost references Bill Moyers's celebrated interviews with Campbell to explain myth as the search for meaning, truth, and significance and equate myth and leadership: "Campbell's understanding of mythology helps explain what has happened to the concept of leadership in the United States. Leadership helps Americans find significance in their search for the meaning of life, helps them reconcile the harsh realities of life. It helps people explain effectiveness and concomitantly allows them to celebrate the people that achieve that effectiveness; the lack of leadership helps them explain ineffectiveness and concomitantly allows them to blame certain people for that ineffectiveness" (pp. 8–9).

What then is the modern hero's journey? Campbell differentiates between two interpretations. As many myths and stories that have been passed down over the centuries, the journey can be assumed to be an *outward journey*, a literal journey whose hero is more easily understood. Perhaps someone named Jason really did steal the Golden Fleece. In contrast, our scientific minds are arrested by such fanciful stories as Prometheus's heroic journey to secure fire for humanity as truth. Although myths allow us to illuminate the concept of the *inner journey*, the word *hero* can be somewhat troubling in this context. In this day and age, we have many conceptions of heroes. A great number of people in our society look up to movie stars and sports figures as personal heroes, whether these individuals have or have not contributed anything of significance to humanity. In the business world, superstar CEOs like Jack Welch or Lee Iacocca are often branded as heroes—at least temporarily; and, in times of despair, those who really do make some personal sacrifice are reported as heroes, such as the New York City firefighters on September 11, 2001. Indeed, sacrifice of some type seems to define the heroic passage. Campbell continues, "If you realize what the problem is—losing yourself, giving yourself to some higher end, or to another—you realize that this itself is the ultimate trial. When we quit thinking primarily about ourselves and our own self-preservation, we undergo a truly heroic transformation of consciousness. And what all myths have to deal with is transformations of consciousness of one kind or another. You have been thinking one way, you now have to think a different way" (1988, pp. 154–155). The heroic journey and transformation go to the heart of a growing sector of leadership studies that seek to lift up and transform the way we work. In a very literal sense, this is leadership not by transaction but by transformation. And it all begins with personal transformation in the form of self-knowledge.

Know Thyself

O wad some Pow'r the giftie gie us
To see oursels as others see us!
   —*Robert Burns, from the poem "To a Louse"*

"Leadership's First Commandment: Know Thyself" claimed the title of the "From the Editor" page of the *Harvard Business Review* (Collingwood, 2001). Reportedly inscribed on the entrance to the Oracle of Delphi, seekers were admonished to "Know Thyself." Increasingly, the leadership literature seems to be addressing this very issue, attending to leadership with heart, leading with soul or the spiritual leader. Parker Palmer claims that the inner world is the true source of reality and power; it is important to take this journey not only so we can live better and happier lives but so we can impact our world in a more positive and life-giving manner. "The best leaders work from a place of integrity in themselves, from their hearts. If they don't, they can't inspire trustful relationships. In the absence of trust, organizations fall apart" (Palmer, 2001, p. 27).

Additionally, Lash argues that top leaders need to take "an inner journey of self-growth to achieve outstanding results for themselves and their organization" (2002, p. 45). Research by Lash and colleagues shows that leaders of successful teams need mental and emotional maturity along with other important leadership aptitudes and competencies. Before leaders can develop others and help their own teams' effectiveness, they first have to understand themselves. Lash and colleagues add, "The journey is the way in which leaders develop socialized power and find new ways to lead and achieve better results for their organization. It is an ancient theme of self-growth. It has been described as a passage from the secure and familiar into the unfamiliar and mysterious, and back again" (p. 45).

Additionally, Scharmer's Theory U addresses the inner journey. "We know a great deal about *what* leaders do and how they do it. But we know very little about the inner place, the source from which they operate. Successful leadership depends on the quality of attention and intention that the leaders bring to any situation" (Scharmer, 2008, p. 52). Scharmer explains that all leaders do the same thing that artists do by creating something new and presenting it to the world (Scharmer, 2007, p. 22); yet the core of leadership deals with how both individuals and groups respond to a given situation. "The essence of leadership is to shift the inner place from which we operate both individually and collectively" (2007, p. 11). Scharmer adds that traveling the U, like the heroic journey, is not often taken in organizations "because it requires an inner journey and hard work" (2008, p. 56).

"Today's visionary leaders echo the most ancient wisdom: To be happy for life, you must first try to know yourself" (Csikszentmihalyi, 2003, p. 19). So how does one go about knowing himself or herself? Csikszentmihalyi describes two paths. The first involves introspection and critical reflection—the philosopher's route. Csikszentmihalyi believes, though, that business leaders in particular consider self-knowledge a means and not an end. He thus illustrates a way of "action" that embraces a core belief that the leader feels can be sustaining, often a belief learned very early in life. Regardless, the road to self-knowledge is a difficult one and involves reflection. Csikszentmihalyi adds, "Knowing oneself is not so much a question of discovering what is present in one's self, but rather of creating who one wants to be" (p. 169). He cites Max DePree's distinction between management and leadership: "Management has a lot to do with answers. But leadership is a function of questions. And the first question for the leader always is: 'Who do we intend to be?' Not 'What are we going to do?' but 'Who do we intend to be?'" (Depree, cited in Csikszentmihalyi, 2003, p. 169).

Choosing the road to self-knowledge is what Campbell might consider a compelling *call*. It is the beginning of the journey, the separation from the known. Gardner and Laskin (1995) concur that it is up to the individual to create a sense of self or identity. Leadership goes a step further. "Leaders who help individuals conceptualize a personal identity perform a crucial function" (Gardner & Laskin, p. 52). Self-knowledge is the starting point of both personal transformation and transformation of others through the leadership process. Though transformational leadership as a school of thought is well known, it is often difficult to see actual transformation in most leadership actions. The hero's journey is the archetype of personal transformation and a timeless lens into the nature of the development of a leader.

The Stages of the Hero's Journey

Campbell's development of the heroic journey is an amazing and complex view of human development. Historically, the heroic journey was based on the three stages of ritual, more specifically of rites of passage, as first explained by van Gennep (1960). The first stage is *separation*, when the initiate is separated from his or her known world. The next stage is *initiation*. In ritual this is the initiatory process or ordeal. The final stage is the *return*, when the initiate returns to the community and is subsequently considered a full-fledged member of society, an adult. "A hero ventures forth from the world of common day into a region of supernatural wonder: fabulous forces are there encountered and a decisive victory is won: the hero comes back from this mysterious adventure with the power to bestow boons on his fellow man" (Campbell, 1968, p. 30). Campbell explains that this quest is not just the basis of myth and folklore but represents a map of journeys taken by humans since the beginning of time. We follow almost predictable paths, though each and every one of us experiences a unique journey. It is a journey of *transformation*.

Carol Pearson has developed insightful work on the journey by examining the archetypes that are at play in each of the stages (1991, 1998). She explains that the importance of the journey and the myth of the hero are links to our past *and* our future. The paradox of our modern lives is that as we continue to blaze paths and create new possibilities, for many of us, our lives and actions feel empty and devoid of spirit. "To transcend this state, we need to feel rooted simultaneously in history and eternity" (1991, p. 2). This concept sheds light upon the need to learn from history while keeping an eye toward the future and the creation of something new. Ultimately, the hero's journey is a path that all leaders must take in one respect or another. "It is about fearlessly leaping off the edge of the known to confront the unknown, and trusting that when the time comes, we will have what we need to face our dragons, discover our treasures, and return to transform the kingdom. It is also about learning to be true to ourselves and live in responsible community with one another" (1991, p. 2).

Pearson explains that the three phases of the journey are replicas of the stages of human psychological development. First the ego is developed (*preparation* in Pearson's model; *separation* in Campbell's), then the soul is encountered (Pearson: *journey*; *initiation*: Campbell), and finally a new and unique sense of self is born (*self*: Pearson; *return*: Campbell). Spreitzer, Quinn, and Fletcher explain the journey with a leadership focus. "The hero's journey is the experience of separating oneself from the increasingly dull and disempowering status quo, initiating the engagement of uncertainty, constructing a new and more efficacious meaning-making system, and then returning self-empowered and empowering to others" (1995, p. 17).

The heroic journey, marked by three major stages, is explicated following. Each hero experiences "a separation from the world, a penetration to some source of power, and a life-enhancing return" (Campbell, 1968, p. 35). These phases are akin to a death and resurrection, with the leader returning as a new person.

Stage 1: Separation

In the separation stage, the hero feels a pull to change. The pull may be self-directed or it may be almost arbitrary. Many people experience this through "wake-up calls" such as a life-threatening illness, a divorce, or the real possibility of losing one's job. Campbell explains that the first step of separation, withdrawal, or detachment represents a shift of emphasis from the external to the internal world of the hero: the inner journey. "The first work of the hero is to retreat from the world scene of secondary effects to those causal zones of the psyche where the difficulties really reside, and there to clarify the difficulties, eradicate them in his own case . . . and break through to the undistorted, direct experience and assimilation of what C.G. Jung called 'the archetypal images'" (1968, pp. 17–18).

Pearson calls this stage the *preparation* and introduces the first four archetypes. These archetypes are responsible for building a healthy ego—a prerequisite for the journey and a necessity for our protection. Both Freud and Jung would agree that we all have an inner child within that bears the scars of our formation. Pearson acknowledges that the Ego's first role is to protect the inner child, while its second and most basic task is to supervise our connection with the outside world. Preparation for the journey requires skills of socialization as well as assertion of our own independent values and drives. This preparation must occur with an eye toward the good of the whole, not as a selfish goal (Pearson, 1991, pp. 30–31).

Stage 2: Initiation

"Answering the call" pushes the hero across the threshold and into the unknown, the beginning of the second stage; this is the part of the journey with which we are most familiar, through stories in books and movies. Heroes must pass through a number of challenges as their mettle is tested until finally they are thrown into the abyss to face their greatest fear. If the hero is successful, he or she gets the boon or gift and is transformed. Much of the literature of the world is based on this phase of the journey. In Pearson's language, this stage is called the *journey*. The four archetypes of the journey help us on the *soul* level as we seek meaning and become *authentic* in the process. "Soul is the part of the psyche that connects us with the eternal and provides a sense of meaning and value in our lives" (Pearson, 1991, p. 38).

Stage 3: Return

The journey does not come to completion until the hero returns with the boon to share it with his or her community or the world. The return in itself can be harrowing, and just because the hero has a gift (often a greater understanding of self) doesn't mean anyone else cares. The journey thus continues even after the hero's transformation. "His second solemn task and deed therefore . . . is to return then to us, transfigured, and teach the lesson he has learned of life renewed" (Campbell, 1968, p. 20). This stage is often the most treacherous, because fully transformed, the hero must attempt to reintegrate into life. He or she may choose not to return at all, may be greeted by contempt and disdain or worse, as it relates to us in contemporary context: "Or if the hero, in the third place, makes his safe and willing return, he may meet with such a blank misunderstanding and disregard from those whom he has come to help that his career will collapse" (Campbell, 1968, p. 37). Nonetheless, returning with one's boon and the intention to serve is the mark of leadership and the choice of a true leader. "Heroism is also not just finding a new truth, but having the courage to act on that vision. That is, in a very practical way, why heroes need to have the courage and care associated with strong ego development and the vision and clarity of mind and spirit that come from having taken their souls' journeys and gained the treasure of their true selves" (Pearson, 1991, p. 3). Transformation occurs with the safe return of the hero.

Additional Questions to Be Answered by the Leader

While I have attempted to draw parallels across personal transformation, the development of a leader, and the hero's journey, it may be prudent, at this juncture, to pose three additional questions that ought to be answered by the leader.

Question 1: Why take the journey?

"The great illusion of leadership is to think that man can be led out of the desert by someone who has never been there" (Nouwen, 1972, p. 72). Heeding the call and taking one's own journey contributes to a level of authenticity and purpose that is difficult to gain without having "been there" as Nouwen says. "The practice of leadership requires, perhaps first and foremost, a sense of purpose—the capacity to find the values that make risk-taking meaningful" (Heifetz, 1994, p. 274). Heifetz explains that it is a sense of purpose that allows us, both as individuals (leaders) and organizations, to step back and analyze the current realities, to see the orienting values, and to make the changes necessary to take corrective action. Purpose provides the ability to discover and create new possibilities that then require a learning strategy.

Perhaps no one tackles the need to develop a learning strategy more elegantly than Peter Vaill. Vaill's take on the need for adaptive thinking comes as a result of *permanent white water* (Vaill, 1996). Permanent white water, he explains, is not external to us. "It is *felt*—as confusion and loss of direction and control, as a gnawing sense of meaninglessness" (Vaill, p. 43). For many, confusion is the setup for heeding the *call* and taking the journey. Vaill emphasizes that learning is how we restore our understanding of the world. We have to be effective learners and understand the importance of lifelong learning. Vaill also concurs with Heifetz on the importance of purpose. Though lots of money and time are spent each year to train and develop leaders, managers, and employees in key skills and qualities, Vaill says there is still a gap. "What is still missing are the core values of the person who would do this thing I am calling purposing. What does that person *care* about? What *matters* to the person? What does the person have genuine, spontaneous, unrehearsed, unmodulated, and unhomogenized energy for?

What is at the core of the person's *being?*" (Vaill, 1998, p. 210).

The leader's journey forces us to face our fears, to clarify our values, and to become effective learners. Why take the journey but to learn at a deep level who we are and what we are made of? When the self-aware leader "knows thyself," he or she becomes a more powerful and effective leader. The journey allows us to discover *purpose* as Vaill and Heifetz explain. Organizations also have a purpose. As Fritz notes, "Organizations, like people, suffer when they are not being true to themselves" (1999, p. 149). Fritz calls this a "spiritual purpose," not in the sense of a religious purpose but more akin to a higher calling that an organization embodies. The organizational purpose can be seen in what excites and motivates, the real values and aspirations embodied as well as the products and services offered. Additionally, much like traveling up the U in Theory U, the potential represented by aligning one's own purpose with that of an organization is very powerful. "For most people, there is a direct match between their own values, aspirations, and sense of purpose and that of the organization. But for most people, this match goes unrecognized. If the match is there, there is a possibility for great mutual benefit—organization and member" (Fritz, 1999, p. 156).

Question 2: How does the journey affect the relationship between leaders and followers?

"The function of leadership is to mobilize people—groups, organizations, societies—to address their toughest problems. Effective leadership addresses problems that require people to move from a familiar but inadequate equilibrium—through disequilibrium—to a more adequate equilibrium. That is, today's complex conditions require acts of leadership that assist people in moving beyond the edge of familiar patterns into the unknown terrain of greater complexity, new learning, and new behaviors . . ." (Parks, 2005, p. 9).

Leadership, as Parks describes, closely follows the heroic journey stage by stage and is a good example of adaptive challenges. Movement through the disequilibrium is not easy work; it is not work that can be tackled by technical or expert knowledge. With adaptive work, there is much at stake— for both the individual as well as the organization. "They ask for more than changes in routine or mere preference. They call for changes of heart and mind—the transformation of long-standing habits and deeply held assumptions and values" (Parks, 2005, p. 10). Leadership is thus essential to help lead other individuals as well as the entire organization or social system through their own hero's journey. Couto and Eken call the march through disequilibrium *innovative democratic leadership* and explain it very clearly: "Innovative democratic leadership moves people to unimagined places first by helping them discover their own talent and gifts, which in turn take them and others to that new and better place. The process of discovery that triggers individual and group change begins with compassion, which means accepting the starting point of people in their effort to reach a better place" (2002, p. 207).

Question 3: Is the journey worth the trouble?

Whether the journey is taken as an individual or as a group, there is no doubt that it is a long and often perilous journey. How, then, is one to get through all the ordeals? We do not live in a time or space where the inner journey is widely discussed, much less actively pursued. Palmer speaks boldly: "Our frequent failure as leaders to deal with our inner lives leaves too many individuals and institutions in the dark" (2000, p. 91). He encourages us to help each other because ultimately there is no way around the journey if we are to be fulfilled and fully functioning. Palmer gives three suggestions for the work on one's inner journey. First, inner work should be valued. It is important to understand that inner work is as real as outer work. It also involves skills that can be developed such as journaling, reflective reading, meditation, and prayer. Second, though inner work is very *personal* it is not necessarily *private*. Inner work can be worked on and shared in different community settings, and one way to share is through coaching. Third, it is important to acknowledge the role fear plays in our lives. Palmer uses the biblical exhortation "Be not afraid" as an example of this shared human struggle. "'Be not afraid' does not mean we cannot *have* fear. Everyone has fear, and people who embrace the call to leadership often find fear abounding. Instead, the words say we do not need to be the fear we have. We do not have to lead from a place of fear, thereby engendering a world in which fear is multiplied" (2000, pp. 93–94).

Palmer's insights lead us to the "uncomfortable" realm of spirituality and the question of what, if anything, it has to do with leadership. Citizens of the United States actively try to practice a separation of church and state, but do we dare consciously bring spirituality into the workplace? Wheatley (2005) believes spirituality to be a necessity. She argues that there is no way to create stability and control for people to feel secure, and it is essential for leaders to develop a relationship with uncertainty and chaos. She explains that the creation of this relationship has always been the work of spiritual teachers, and as leaders we must now enter this domain to be successful. Wheatley describes several "principles" that explain why spiritual work is essential: Life is uncertain and cyclical. Meaning is what motivates us and service is what brings us joy. Courage comes from our hearts, and we are all interconnected. We can count on human goodness but still require peace of mind (p. 126).

Buddhist teacher and writer Jack Kornfield (1993) explains the need to include spiritual life and vision in our being and doing. He clarifies that to be helpful, spirituality needs to be grounded in personal experience. That experience is rooted in a practice or a discipline. "Until a person chooses one discipline and commits to it, how can a deep understanding of themselves and the world be revealed to them? Spiritual work requires sustained practice and a commitment to look very deeply into ourselves and the world around us . . ." (p. 33). Couto and Eken remind us that successful leadership involves working both with the self and with others. Leadership finds direction through some form of internal and personal change. Personal change is often precipitated by the initiation of change efforts, or as they eloquently state, "Change efforts change the agents of change" (2002, p. 208). Committing to a change effort, in turn, creates the confidence necessary to take the journey. Couto and Eken add, "The confidence of leadership does not spring from the certainty about the definition of a problem or its solution—this is the confidence of the expert. The confidence of leadership comes from the very process and values of adaptive work. The confidence of innovative democratic leadership exudes from a certainty that expressing human bonds and the responsibility that we have for each other embody the highest human moral values. Efforts to bring social practice into line with those values express the highest form of human activity, whatever their shortcomings" (pp. 199–200).

Conclusion

The expression and embodiment of personal and collective values in working toward the uplifting of our spirit or consciousness in the pursuit of both individual and communal transformation is the goal toward which leadership ultimately strives. While perhaps appearing simplistic, the journey is not direct but circuitous. It is not linear, but cyclical in nature. While every voyage begins with a new *call*, the hero's journey does not end with each *return*. It is a process of growth that envelops and demands constant change. The journey teaches us to seek to understand and embrace this change. Whether it is an individual on his or her own heroic journey or a group, team, or organization traveling the U, we return to the place we began—the quest for understanding and the search for meaning, a journey of change and transformation—the heroic journey.

References

Campbell, J. (1968). *The hero with a thousand faces* (2nd ed.). Princeton, NJ: Princeton University Press.

Campbell, J. (1988). *Historical atlas of world mythology*. New York: Perennial Library.

Collingwood, H. (December, 2001). Editorial: Leadership's first commandment: Know thyself. *Harvard Business Review, 79*(11), 8.

Couto, R. A., & Eken, S. C. (2002). *To give their gifts: Health, community, and democracy* (1st ed.). Nashville: Vanderbilt University Press.

Csikszentmihalyi, M. (2003). *Good business: Leadership, flow, and the making of meaning*. New York: Viking.

Eliot, T. S. (1952). *The complete poems and plays 1909–1950*. New York: Harcourt, Brace & Co.

Fritz, R. (1999). *The path of least resistance for managers: Designing organizations to succeed* (1st ed.). San Francisco: Berrett-Koehler.

Gardner, H., & Laskin, E. (1995). *Leading minds: An anatomy of leadership*. New York: Basic Books.

Heifetz, R. A. (1994). *Leadership without easy answers*. Cambridge, MA: Belknap Press of Harvard University Press.

Kornfield, J. (1993). *A path with heart: A guide through the perils and promises of spiritual life*. New York: Bantam Books.

Lash, R. (2002). Top leadership taking the inner journey. *Ivey Business Journal, 66*(5), 44–48.

Nouwen, H.J.M. (1972). *The wounded healer; ministry in contemporary society* (1st ed.). Garden City, NY: Doubleday.

Palmer, P. (2001, Fall). Leadership and the inner journey. *Leader to Leader,* 26–33.

Palmer, P. J. (2000). *Let your life speak: Listening for the voice of vocation*. San Francisco: Jossey-Bass.

Parks, S. D. (2005). *Leadership can be taught: A bold approach for a complex world*. Boston: Harvard Business School Press.

Pearson, C. (1991). *Awakening the heroes within: Twelve archetypes to help us find ourselves and transform our world*. San Francisco: HarperSanFrancisco.

Pearson, C. (1998). *The hero within: Six archetypes we live by* (3rd ed.). San Francisco: HarperSanFrancisco.

Rost, J. C. (1991). *Leadership for the twenty-first century*. New York: Praeger.

Scharmer, C. O. (2007). *Theory U: Leading from the emerging future* (1st ed.). Cambridge, MA: Society for Organizational Learning.

Scharmer, C. O. (2008, Winter). Uncovering the blind spot of leadership. *Leader to Leader,* 52–59.

Spreitzer, G., Quinn, R., & Fletcher, J. (1995). Excavating the paths of meaning, renewal, and empowerment. *Journal of Management Inquiry, 4*(1), 16–39.

Vaill, P. B. (1996). *Learning as a way of being: Strategies for survival in a world of permanent white water* (1st ed.). San Francisco: Jossey-Bass.

Vaill, P. B. (1998). *Spirited leading and learning: Process wisdom for a new age* (1st ed.). San Francisco: Jossey-Bass.

van Gennep, A. (1960). *The rites of passage* [Rites de passage.]. Chicago: University of Chicago Press.

Wheatley, M. J. (2005). *Finding our way: Leadership for an uncertain time* (1st ed.). San Francisco: Berrett-Koehler.

Transformation in Practice

Wu Feng

Mark Nepo

The way that heat allows ice to thaw and irrigate the earth, our capacity to embody what we know—our quiet need to bring what lives within into accord with how we meet the days—this ancient act of integrity allows Love to show itself as the deepest sort of gravity.

There was a quiet man whose life-changing moment of such courage is inspiring. He was Wu Feng, a Manchurian diplomat of the 1700s posted with an Aboriginal tribe in the outskirts of Taiwan. Wu Feng befriended the Aboriginal chief, whose tribe beheaded one of its members every year as a form of sacrifice.

Each year Wu Feng pleaded with all of his compassion and reverence for life that the chief put an end to this custom. The chief would listen respectfully as Wu Feng would plead, and then, after listening and bowing, the chief would summon the chosen tribe member and, without hesitation, behead him.

Finally, after living with the tribe for twenty-five years, Wu Feng once more pleaded with the chief to stop this senseless killing. But this time, when the tribe member was called forth, Wu Feng took his place and said, "If you will kill this time, it will be me."

The chief stared long into his friend's eyes and, having grown to love Wu Feng, he could not kill him. From that day, the practice of beheading stopped.

Of course, Wu Feng could have been killed, but his courage shows us that, at a certain point, how we live inside takes priority. At a certain point for each of us, talk evaporates and words cannot bring Love into the open. Only the soul's presence coming from us can attract the soul's presence in others. In the end, it is not enough to think what we know. We must live it. For only by living it can Love show itself as the greatest principle.

From *Facing the Lion, Being the Lion*, Mark Nepo. San Francisco: Conari Press, 2007, p. 252.

Authentic Accountability

Tapping the Power of the Infinite Game

Jay Gordon Cone

> There are at least two kinds of games. One could
> be called finite, the other infinite.
> A finite game is played for the purpose of winning;
> an infinite game is played for the purpose of
> continuing the play.
> —*James Carse (1986, p. 3)*

At a medical device company in February 2009, I was facilitating a leadership development program for high-potential leaders. The program included a computer-based simulation that allowed teams of participants to develop business acumen and general management skills by operating a simulated technology company over three quarters compressed into three days. A participant who had just learned about the financial objectives for the simulation asked in a very direct way, "What does it take to be the winning team?" While everyone enjoyed a cathartic laugh, grateful that someone blurted out the question on everyone's mind, I was having an internal debate about how to respond.

Perhaps because I'd been preoccupied with thoughts about the state of our global economy, I summoned up the courage to confront rather than deflect the question. "What does it take to win?" I repeated. "I guess that depends on which game you're playing. To win the finite game, you'll need to end up with the highest market share, most significant increase in customer satisfaction, and deliver at least 25 percent pre-tax operating profit by the end of the third quarter." At this point, it seemed to me that most of the participants felt satisfied by the answer, but I was just getting warmed up.

"On the other hand," I paused dramatically, "you can choose to participate in the simulation as an infinite player. If you choose to play the infinite game, winning becomes irrelevant." A few eyes started to roll. Others seemed genuinely confused by the suggestion that winning might be irrelevant. I ignored the reactions and soldiered on. "Instead, you'll be focused on how to integrate what you learn over the next several days back on the job. You'll experiment with the variables of a complex business without worrying about real-world consequences, other than a bruised ego, when we compare each team's results. You'll resist the temptation to slash costs before the final round and, instead, attempt to create lasting value through innovation even if your decisions don't pay off by the time we stop tracking results." I wondered if anyone else in the room had made the connection between treating the simulation as nothing more than a system of variables to be optimized and treating our organizations and our financial markets as nothing more than a system of variables to be optimized. The participant who had asked the question in the first place raised his hand again. I called on him expectantly. "Did you say 20 percent or 25 percent pre-tax profit?"

School as a Finite Game and School as an Infinite Game

Lately I've been thinking a lot about how much Carse's elegant dialectic explains our behavior and approach to a great many things. Early in life we figured out that people with power and authority are keeping score on us and they reward us based on the measure of our achievements. How we value the rewards that others have the authority to dole out has a lot to do with whether we participate as finite or infinite players.

As students, for example, we play the finite game of school when we focus our attention on the goals created by those with the authority to write the rules and define "winning." Our energy is directed toward completing coursework, competing for the highest grade point average, comparing test scores against the other players, and getting into the right schools. Infinite play, because it strives to perpetuate itself, means we focus on the process of education rather than the outcomes. We follow our curiosity, become lifelong learners, and intentionally seek out opportunities to start new subjects or pursue new lines of inquiry. The finite player in the education system focuses on finishing each game (this course, that school) with the best scores. The infinite player in the education system focuses on how to extend education beyond the formal passages from one level to the next.

A student who ignores the rules of the finite game never graduates. He has no desire to cross a finish line. He drifts from subject to subject. He follows his curiosity but stops short at the difficult hurdles because he sees no value in surmounting obstacles to satisfy someone else's definition of success. It seems that we can't abandon the finite game completely if we want to be productive citizens.

However, a student who loses touch with the infinite game sees his or her curiosity atrophy. Throughout the semester, the obsessively finite player asks, "Will this be on the final?"—code for "Do I have to pay attention to this?" In the end, an exclusive focus on what it takes to complete the class renders everything else about the subject irrelevant. The finite student-player leaves school with a winning GPA and no ability to interpret the complexities of the world, to think creatively or analytically when faced with a challenge, or to deal effectively with change. Eventually, the student who overemphasizes the finite game of school loses the capacity and motivation to learn. "Why should I keep learning if my mastery of a subject is not being measured or rewarded?"

Work as a Finite Game and Work as an Infinite Game

In the context of performance management, contrasting the perspective of work as a finite game and work as an infinite game amounts to defining what it means for someone to be successful. Business has been genetically encoded to equate success with measurable outcomes and winning. We compete for market share. We participate in well-defined time periods: months, quarters, and fiscal years. We create goals and measures so that we can compare, contrast, and rank individuals, groups, and organizations.

It may seem sacrilegious, or at least nonsensical, to suggest that in business success might be something other than winning. With all due respect to Vince Lombardi, winning is not the only thing. It makes for great locker room speeches, but surely Lombardi wouldn't choose to play a season against, say, only high school football teams in order to guarantee a win. Even in professional sports, arguably the most finite of finite games, elements of the infinite game penetrate like willful blades of grass through cracks in the sidewalk: the joy of being pushed to play beyond your capability, the experience of a cohesive team effort, the connection to an activity that you once played for the sheer pleasure of it.

Businesses exist, according to conventional wisdom, to generate a profit. If profit making defines the activity of business, we shouldn't be surprised by the ascendancy of scorekeeping as the gauge of success. Interesting enough, the father of management theory, Peter Drucker, believed that "the purpose of a business is to create and keep a customer" (1954, p. 37). Drucker's definition hints at the possibility of an infinite game beneath the surface of the concrete profit-and-loss statement. Creating and keeping customers, after all, is an activity that perpetuates itself.

How Winning the Finite Game Can Undermine Authentic Accountability

We crave employees who "act like owners" or demonstrate an "entrepreneurial spirit," so we align business goals with compensation—a definitively finite way to play. We define winning with measurable outcomes within a fixed time frame and then release the players to do whatever it takes. We expect them to play by the rules, but we're mesmerized by the scoreboard and occasionally miss attempts to "leverage" the rules on behalf of improving the score; if it doesn't say you can't, then you can, right? Our attempt to increase accountability by linking rewards with results actually undermines our desire to create a culture of entrepreneurship and ownership. Instead, our judgment gets disabled by an unconscious myopia that makes deceptive accounting practices and loaning money to unqualified borrowers seem like reasonable ideas.

Real entrepreneurs, it turns out, are driven by passion and persistence—two stubbornly immeasurable traits. Of course, entrepreneurs want to "put points on the board." The difference is that the final score for the entrepreneur isn't the end of the game; it's the jumping-off point to see what more is possible. To the infinite player, the score provides data about progress and potential. Even when it's working perfectly, a performance management system that focuses on finite goals limits your organization to what's expected and dooms your leaders to apply their energies to what someone else wants of them. We breed leaders who are passionate about winning, not about playing. We breed leaders who wait for others to define success for them. We breed leaders who are persistent until they can blame someone or something else for coming up short. While we decry a general lack of accountability, we simultaneously create dependence by limiting the field of play and narrowing the definition of success. More than twenty years ago, Peter Block, in *The Empowered*

Manager, made a similar point by contrasting the "Bureaucratic Cycle" and the "Entrepreneurial Cycle." Block (1987) wrote, "In many ways, organizations unintentionally encourage people to choose to maintain what they have, to be cautious and dependent" (p. 20).

Managing Infinite Players, Leadership in the Infinite Game

It's not just that our compensation and performance management systems are inefficient and ineffective; they actually punish the infinite player who is the true entrepreneur and reward the finite player who won't make a move until he or she knows whether the move will pay off. Suddenly, we look around in amazement that no one takes initiative or demonstrates any accountability. To whom or to what would we have them be accountable? The truly accountable workers are playing the infinite game; they don't look to their managers to impose the rules and criteria for winning. The truly accountable, infinite players will naturally choose to do what's in the long-term interest of the business, because they place a higher priority on continuing play than on winning.

Reawakening our inner infinite player requires understanding the characteristics of infinite performance as distinct from the characteristics of finite performance, as described in Table 7.1.

Here's the good news: you don't need to incent the infinite player. Here's the bad news: you can't incent the infinite player. Infinite play occurs naturally when leaders unleash the potential of people whose work makes a meaningful difference in the world.

Conclusion: Lead Infinitely and Manage Finitely

Infinite players who ignore the finite attributes of the game may never realize their full potential. Obsession with the infinite

Table 7.1   The Finite Player Mind-Set versus the Infinite Player Mind-Set

Characteristics of Finite Performance	Characteristics of Infinite Performance
What interests my boss fascinates me	I am my boss
Success = results	Success = finding new ways to play
Work or Life	Work is Life
I must win	I must improve
Undermine and disrupt the competition	Support and learn from all the players
The rules define the game	Ignore rules that no longer serve the players
Do what's rewarded	Do what's valuable

game becomes quixotic. Any level of performance satisfies the leader who overemphasizes the infinite game. The mantra of the leader who refuses to step into the arena of the finite game is "que será, será."

Management is a finite game; leadership is an infinite game. We count on leadership to temper the attitude of "win at all costs" with gentle reminders of the nobler pursuits. If we allow leaders who are obsessed with the finite game to run our businesses, we shouldn't be surprised that they expend their innovative energies on ways to tinker with the scoreboard instead of inventing new ways to play the game; and when the stadium clears, we're left bankrupt in more ways than one.

References

Block, P. (1987). *The empowered manager.* San Francisco: Jossey-Bass.
Carse, J. P. (1986). *Finite and infinite games.* New York: Ballantine.
Drucker, P. (1954). *The practice of management.* New York: Harper & Row.

What Art Offers Leadership

Looking Beneath the Surface

Skye Burn

> If you have the idea that an artist is not a
> decidedly practical person, get over it.
> —*Robert Henri (1923, p. 190)*

Imagine a meeting in the U.S. president's office. An urgent situation has arisen. The president has called in expert advisers to help assess the situation and figure out how to respond. Clustered in the Oval Office with serious expressions tightening their faces are trusted legal advisers, economic advisers, political advisers, and military advisers. Privately, before the meeting, the president sought religious counsel.

Who is missing from this scenario?

Artists are missing. The president's team of expert advisers does not include artists. Few leaders turn to artists for advice in responding to situations that arise in their communities and organizations. Society tends to value artists for the objects and entertainment they create, not for the knowledge and experience they have gained through the process of creating art. The practice of art is generally considered irrelevant in solving "real-world" problems, and artists are not known for their practicality.

Today humanity is facing life-threatening situations: climate change, pollution, terrorism, economic instability, religious conflict, food insecurity, water shortages. These situations are not entirely amenable to political, economic, and military solutions. They require creative solutions. It seems that artists could be a valuable resource in developing creative solutions.

In 2009, Michael Kaiser, president of the Kennedy Center in New York City, toured the United States speaking with leaders of arts organizations about how to survive the economic crisis and drastically reduced funding for the arts. The thrust of his message was we need to be much clearer about the value of what art offers.

The question is not only how we can get the world to see more clearly the value of what art offers. The question is also how artists can themselves recognize the value and relevance of their knowledge and experience with respect to the challenging situations facing humanity.

The Flow Project

A few years ago three artists were sitting around a kitchen table wondering how they could help resolve the difficult situations facing humanity. The artists wanted to contribute, but they were not sure what they had to offer. How could artists make a meaningful contribution to solving world problems beyond the traditional role of art in providing humanity with a means of soul searching and self-reflection?

After several kitchen table conversations, which included experiential thought processes with crayons and pastels, the artists began to sense an emerging possibility. They realized leaders listen to economists who explain the principles of economics and economic forces that shape the world, and leaders listen to political strategists who help them understand the political forces at work in various situations. Leaders would not imagine addressing a complex situation without awareness of the political forces at work. To artists the world of art is just as real as the world of economics or the world of politics. The question that came to the artists was, "How can we get leaders to understand the principles of art and the artistic-creative forces that shape the world?" On some level they felt intuitively that leaders need to understand the principles of art and artistic-creative forces to generate creative solutions to the situations we face today. In other words, they felt leaders need to learn to "think like artists."

After sitting with the question for a while, one of the artists originated a simple plan. It involved engaging artists in a deep inquiry to identify principles of art and artistic practices common to the artistic experience across mediums, working with well-positioned allies in the field of leadership education to translate the principles of art into principles of leadership and leadership practices, and presenting the offering to the global community.

The plan was implemented and The Flow Project was established as a nonprofit corporation in 2008. The Flow Project mission is to give leaders access to knowledge and experience that artists possess and give artists recognition for the value of their knowledge and experience. The Flow Project is centered in Bellingham, Washington, but artists and leadership educators beyond Bellingham are participating.

While the inspiration for The Flow Project originated in the arts community, the justification comes from within the field of leadership. In his Foreword to Otto Scharmer's *Theory U: Leading from the Future as It Emerges*, Peter Senge suggests, "The key to addressing the multiple unfolding crises of our time" lies in learning how to access "knowledge deeply imbedded in the creative arts" and artistic mastery (2007, p. xi). The World Commission on Culture and Development report, *Our Creative Diversity*, issued by UNESCO, states, "The notion of creativity can no longer be restricted to the arts. It must be applied across the full spectrum of human problem-solving" (World Commission on Culture and Development, 1995). In "Social Creativity as an Heroic Path in World Crisis," Michael Ray notes, "The world is in crisis—filled with danger and opportunity. The danger is the end of our existence. The opportunity is for a new kind of creativity, a co-creation based on a new level of consciousness. We have to get into the flow of the process of the world as it is transformed" (1999, p. 296).

The name for The Flow Project was chosen on the basis of multiple meanings. In geology, *flow* refers to the ability to transform under pressure without breaking apart. In art, *flow* means the work has smooth continuity; it flows. *Flow* also refers to the state artists are in when they are creating works of art, sometimes described as being in the "zone" or "groove." In leadership and organizational development, the flow state is generally called "alignment"; it occurs when the members of a group are working with a sense of common purpose and shared vision. In *Synchronicity: The Inner Path of Leadership*, Joseph Jaworski observes that alignment "happens when people in a group actually start to function as a whole" (1998, p. 6). In *The Managerial Moment of Truth*, Bruce Bodaken and Robert Fritz explain, "Alignment is a requisite for the organization. Without it, managers pull in different directions. With it, managers have an overall organizing principle that motivates them to pull together" (2006, p. 147). Mihaly Csikszentmihalyi has produced the most thorough analysis of the flow state. He notes the flow state occurs when "everyone is investing psychic energy in a joint goal" (1997, p. 112). Further, Csikszentmihalyi observes, "It is the full involvement of flow, rather than happiness, that makes for excellence in life" (p. 32).

Underlying The Flow Project is the idea that artists have knowledge and experience that can be applied in creating organizations and communities that operate in the flow mode. Resolving the life-threatening situations humanity faces in the world today requires concerted action undertaken with a sense of common purpose and shared vision. The Flow Project offers theory and practical techniques that can be used to attain alignment in organizations, institutions, systems, and the global community.

The work of The Flow Project has attracted strong supporters, including board members, volunteer staff, dozens of artists who are engaged in the artist inquiry, well-positioned allies in the field of leadership education, university students doing related research, and international advisers on different continents. The Flow Project is scalable; meaning from a small beginning in Bellingham the artist inquiry can continue to expand to other locations as interest grows. In addition, the principles and practices of art that have been identified and applied are proving useful in producing the flow state in large-scale organizations as well as small-scale operations. The work began locally but it is attracting interest nationally and internationally.

Principles of Art That Apply to Leadership

> One can explain the development of human
> culture only by understanding the process of
> creating a work of art.
> —*Lewis Mumford* (1956, p. 13)

Changes in global culture, developments in the world of ideas, and the transformation of consciousness are forcing leaders to redefine their roles, learn new skills, and develop new capacities.

Globalization and the Internet have transformed global culture, producing a global community with economic ties and a communication "grapevine" that provides immediate feedback and information sharing worldwide. With the increasing interconnectedness and the sense of living in "closer quarters," we are becoming increasingly sensitive to our religious, ethnic, and cultural diversity. The wider and deeper exposure to our common humanity and the growing familiarity are forcing leaders to learn to act in the common interest while simultaneously advancing the interests of their separate organizations and communities. Leaders must learn how to foster the identities of their separate nations, organizations, and groups while simultaneously fostering and supporting the emergence of a global identity. Understanding the principles of art may give leaders such know-how.

In the world of ideas, the advent of systems thinking— thinking in terms of the whole system—and the idea of self-organization undermine the hierarchical notion that leaders must remain "in control" and "on top" of situations. Margaret Wheatley observes, "Self-organizing systems have the capacity to create for themselves the aspects of organization that we thought leaders had to provide" (2005, p. 26). Today leaders are asking, If organizations, communities, and the dynamic of culture are *self-organizing*, what is the role of leaders? Further, if leaders let go of the idea of being in control, how do we get past the fear of losing control of situations and the fear of people being out of control? Leaders need insight into how to lead humanity into a world beyond fear, which the experience of art may provide.

The global transformation of consciousness, from the consciousness of isolation and separation to the consciousness of transpersonal interconnectedness and interrelatedness, has created a problem for leadership. Becoming conscious of the ways in which our actions affect the whole system has brought home the realization that we must collectively change our ways, and leaders are at the forefront in figuring out how to make the necessary adjustments. Further, the systemic structures (organizations, institutions, governments) that support the activity of the global community are still geared to the old mentality of separation. The systemic structures need to be revised to accommodate the new mode of operation based on the consciousness of connection. Here, The Flow Project participants believe that art-based leadership practices and strategies can greatly assist with leadership for transformation.

Specific Things That Art Offers Leadership

Seeing New Possibilities

Robin Pogrebin of the *New York Times* quotes Jim Leach, director of the U.S. National Endowment for the Humanities, "Our culture is shaped by the arts and humanities often more than it is by politics. And in difficult times the arts, sciences, and humanities vastly increase in significance. And this is one of those times" (Pogrebin, 2009). Theater director Anne Bogart adds, "The arts are most indispensable in the midst of cultural, political, and scientific paradigm shifts. It is at these moments that risk, innovation, expression, and dramatic leaps of imagination are critical and necessary" (2007, p. 112). Poet T. S. Eliot observes, "Art serves us best precisely at that point where it can shift our sense of what is possible" (quoted in Bogart, 2007, p. 121). The thinking of Leach, Bogart, and Eliot is linked to what Sharon Daloz Parks, a leadership educator and ally of The Flow Project, holds as a major contribution of artists: artists can "assist us in seeing the connections among things and in building a systemic awareness—a larger consciousness that helps the group to find the room in which to move to a new place" (2005, p. 224).

Feeling Comfortable Letting Go

Leaders are sensing the need to cease being controlling. Joseph Jaworski observes, "If we are to participate in the unfolding process of the universe, we must let life *flow* through us, rather than attempt to *control* life" (1998, p. 44). Artists can help leaders understand how to let go and find the "right balance." Novelist Madeline L'Engle observes, "In the act of creativity, the artist lets go of self-control which he normally clings to, and is open to riding the wind" (cited in Matanovic, 1985, p. 91). Bogart adds, "If your work is too controlled, it has no life. If it is too chaotic, no one can see or hear it" (2001, p. 132).

Developing a Sense of Common Purpose and Shared Meaning

Leaders realize a sense of common purpose is crucial for organizational vitality and community cohesion. Jon Hawkes explains, "A shared sense of meaning and purpose is the single attitude most strongly associated with community well being" (2004, p. 13), and a "society makes (or discovers) meaning through its arts" (p. 24). Kouzes and Posner observe that leaders enunciate "the meaning and significance of the organization's work so that people understand their own important role in creating it," and transformational leadership requires a "communion of purpose" (2002, pp. 152–153). John Kotter observes the "biggest payoff" in transforming organizations and making change happen occurs when we "act in concert with others" (2005, p. 134).

Developing Unity without Eroding Diversity

Art exemplifies an integrative function. Christopher Alexander explains, "A work of art has life more or less to the extent that *every* single one of its component parts and spaces is whole, well-shaped and positive" (2002, p. 173). Robert Kaupelis observes a drawing or painting "works" when "it's composed, it has structure; it makes a statement; it's unified; it's well-organized; it's harmonious throughout; it's well-designed; there's a total integration of parts; nothing is superfluous; everything holds together" (1980, p. 39).

Instilling a Sense of Order Instead of Disorder in the Global Community

Looking through the lens of art can help leaders see the existence of order in the world. Henri notes, "Art is the noting of the existence of order throughout the world" (1923, p. 144). Oscar Kokoschka echoes: the task of the artist is to "organize the chaos of the visible world in patterns from which some meaning can emerge" (cited in Roditi, 1980, p. 86), which relates to Wheatley's (2005) observation that emergent patterns in self-organizing systems reveal the existence of underlying order based on shared meaning and purpose.

Appreciating the Value of Resistance

Leaders often encounter resistance to their initiatives. Artists can help leaders appreciate the creative value of resistance. In art, resistance generates energy that fuels the creative process, and working through resistance serves to deepen the experience of meaning. Bogart observes, "The opposition between a force pushing towards action and another force holding back is translated into visible and feel-able energy in space and time. This struggle with the obstacle in turn induces discord and imbalance. The attempt to restore harmony from this agitated state generates yet more energy. This battle is, in itself, the creative act" (2001, p. 148). McNiff adds, "The difficulties are always the most important ingredients in the total picture of a creative experience" (1998b, p. 13).

Seeing beneath the Surface

Leaders pay attention to undercurrents in their organizations and they seek hidden opportunities. Artists can help leaders detect the deepest undercurrents in the dynamic of contemporary culture. Stanley Kunitz notes, "Poetry explores depths of thought and feeling that civilization requires for its survival" (in Moyers, 1999, p. 41).

Identifying Design Features That Create a World where Human Affairs Flow

From the artist's perspective, the goal of art is not necessarily the created product. Rather, Henri explains, "The goal back of every work of art is the attainment of a state of being, a state of high functioning, a more than ordinary moment of existence" (1923, p. 159). Abraham Maslow calls the state of being "peak experience" (1970) and Csikszentmihalyi calls it "flow" (1996, 1997). Keith Sawyer, a student of Csikszentmihalyi, identifies ten "conditions" or design features of organizations, teams, and groups that operate in the flow mode:

1. A common goal focuses the group activity, yet the goal must be "open-ended enough" for "creativity to emerge."
2. There is "deep listening" to what is emerging.
3. The work environment allows the group to concentrate "on the natural progress emerging from members' work, not on meeting a deadline set by management."
4. The "participants feel in control" yet are "willing to defer to the emergent flow" of the group process.
5. The group members are able to "submerge their egos to the group mind, to balance their own voices with deep listening."
6. All participants "play equal roles in the collective creation process."
7. The participants have developed a level of familiarity and have practice working together.
8. There is the opportunity for spontaneous communication and
9. The opportunity to build on what others have created.
10. Every activity is treated as a learning experience. (Sawyer, 2007, pp. 39–57)

Barbara Marx Hubbard adds, "When we are in the flow there is a feeling of being organized by the deeper pattern rather than by having to make things happen by will and linear planning alone. . . . There is a sense of effortless although everyone is working very hard" (1998, p. 155).

Noting how some of these features are present and some are missing in the world today, purposefully instituting the features where possible, and recognizing the challenges humanity faces in transitioning to the flow state will give global community leaders guidance in creating systems, organizations, and communities that accommodate the new state of being.

The Flow Project believes artists have knowledge and experience, in these and other areas, that leaders need in order to create organizations and communities that run smoothly. At the very least, we feel the urgent need for creative solutions to the life-threatening situations the global community is facing warrants exploration of the ways that art can inform leadership.

Structure of the Flow Inquiry: A Multiphase Approach to Artists' Knowing

> Artists can respond to the issues that confront us
> culturally and take them to a deeper level of
> consciousness, where the challenge is not
> polarized, but is resolved internally. Works that
> come from such a transmutation do not simply
> mirror or magnify the challenges, but demonstrate
> the solution
> —*Milenko Matanovic (1985, p. 199)*

An objective of The Flow Project is that leaders should seek knowledge that artists possess. For many artists, the knowledge is second nature and instinctual and has never been articulated. Thus, the process of accessing and verbalizing the knowledge is a process of self-discovery and self-recognition for the artists as well as for leaders who benefit from the artists' way of knowing.

In crafting the artist inquiry, the Flow Process Team (persons who have accepted responsibility for the data collection and processing) has developed a systematic approach with enough built-in controls to make the results useful, an approach that meets rigorous standards of academic excellence while permitting the artists to participate as full partners in shaping and directing the inquiry. Artists are acknowledged as the experts; the success of the inquiry depends on them to help identify and clarify the questions that need to be asked in order to access their knowledge. Further, as the artists need to stay within their comfort zone to feel comfortable sharing their knowledge and experience, they are the arbiters when they feel the inquiry is drifting too far in the direction of lifeless abstraction or reductionism.

Rather than predetermining where the inquiry will lead with preset questions, the Flow Process Team settled on a methodological structure for the inquiry that allows an emergent line of questioning to develop. In *Art-Based Research*, Shaun McNiff explains, "Since the fruits of the creative process tend to arrive unexpectedly, it is essential to establish a methodological structure which will define and contain the data within a purposeful context" (1998a, p. 147). The methodological structure of inquiry serves the purpose of The Flow Project by allowing the project to find its own momentum and develop a life of its own, for a fundamental principle of art is the knowledge that a work of art has an autonomous life of its own (McNiff, 1998b).

The Flow Project is designed to accommodate artist inquiries in multiple locations. The data collected from every inquiry session is sent to the Flow Process Team for processing, and the results fed back to the artist inquiry, producing a feedback loop that informs the ongoing inquiry. In each location, the team that conducts the inquiry includes a coordinator and/or facilitator, recorders, and artists. The Flow Process Team interviews and approves the coordinators and facilitators, who must complete an orientation and agree to operate within the parameters of The Flow Project. The facilitators select the recorders and artists following established criteria. The artists must complete an application and interview process. The inquiry is limited to experienced artists, and the aim is to engage artists who work in different media and who represent diverse cultural backgrounds.

The Knowledge from Artists Is Generated, Collected, and Processed in Phases

During the initial phase of the artist inquiry, an "art-based research" method is used to collect data. *Art-based research* is "defined by its use of the arts as objects of inquiry as well as modes of investigation" (McNiff, 1998a, p. 15). Artists understand the principles of art through working with their media, and the initial inquiry has a strong experiential component. Otherwise, the artists could be cut off from the source of their knowledge, which would truncate the inquiry. Recognizing what the practice of art offers leadership is opening artists to a new dimension of the artistic experience. Including an experiential component allows the artists to begin exploring the social relevance of their practice without losing their grounding. The artist's way of knowing is grounded in the ability to sense the "energy of the subject matter" (Allen, 1995, p. 21), and that sense of the energy can be occluded if the structure of the inquiry does not invite and nourish subjective experience.

The artist inquiry sessions are recorded using a combination of audio and video recording, still photographs, graphic recording, and written notes. In addition to interviews and reflections during artist inquiry, data on the artistic experience is collected from books, articles, blogs, and Web sites, and other input.

In all locations, the artist inquiry begins at the same starting point. In the first session, the facilitator explains the purpose of The Flow Project and the inquiry structure and methodology. The artists are then asked to respond to a set of three questions:

1. Given the purpose, what is one thing you would like to see in the artist's inquiry?
2. Why is this important to you?
3. Why is this important to the communal work?

The responses are recorded and sent to the Flow Process Team in Bellingham. The team processes the data using the grounded theory method, supported by a computer program, and returns the results to the facilitator in the form of a narrative report. The report identifies and prioritizes themes that emerged from the responses, and the most salient theme becomes the basis of the next inquiry session.

The Flow Process Team uses the grounded theory method to process the data collected from the artist inquiry. Grounded theory is a research method that formulates theory from the ground up rather than from the top down (Glaser & Strauss, 1965, 1967; Strauss & Corbin, 1990). Rather than beginning with a theory or hypothesis that the researcher sets out to prove or disprove, grounded theory begins with accumulating data about an experience through interviews and other sources. The theory emerges through a systematic process of sorting the data, seeing emerging themes, and analyzing patterns to identify basic principles. Often, the final theory is presented in the form of a narrative.

After the initial artist inquiry has identified themes and basic principles and the artists are accustomed to thinking in terms of the social relevance of their practice, the narrative reports from all the sessions are consolidated and sent to the leadership educators allied with The Flow Project. The leadership educators examine the findings and develop a refined set of questions to present to master artist forums. The artists for the master artist forums are selected from the artists who participated in the initial inquiry, based on the acuity of their reflection on the artistic experience, their ability to communicate, and their understanding of and commitment to The Flow Project objectives. Each forum consists of artists who work in different media and who represent diverse cultural backgrounds.

The master artist forums consider the questions developed by the leadership educators in a facilitated dialogue, which does not include an experiential component. Again, the responses are recorded and sent to the Flow Process Team for processing. After the process team has processed the data and produced the narrative report, the report is returned to the artists for review. After the artist review, the process team makes adjustments and then relays the report to the leadership educators. When the final report from the artist inquiry is ready to present to the leadership educators, the artists and leadership educators convene in a face-to-face meeting to share and exchange ideas, experiences, and observations. After the meeting, the leadership educators translate the principles and practices of art into principles and practices of leadership and disseminate the learning through their teaching, publications, and leadership practices, attributing The Flow Project.

The dates for the master artist forums and the face-to-face meeting have not yet been set. The Flow Project is still developing momentum, and it has a life of its own. The artist inquiry is an emergent process, which is expanding to new locations as interest in the project grows. The ultimate aim of the artist inquiry and artist forums is *theoretical saturation*, meaning the inquiry has reached the point where it is no longer turning up any new data. Due to the organic nature of the inquiry, it is impossible to predict when the goal of theoretical saturation will be achieved.

Closing

Art is a way of knowing. An artist does not know ahead of time what the work will reveal. A work of art that is truly alive captures the spirit of something in the snare of eternity, and part of the beauty in art is the sense of vulnerability evoked by the fragile contrast between the temporal medium and the timeless essence the work embodies.

The Flow Project is a communal work. Many people are contributing in diverse ways to the life of the work, helping the project grow and giving form to the vision. As long as people continue to bring forward new pieces, new aspects of the work will be revealed. It is too early to say exactly where the work will lead or what it will ultimately reveal. The one thing that can be said with certainty is the people involved in The Flow Project sense they are "onto something," and they are willing to invest their time and energy in The Project because it seems the artists' way of knowing may give leaders the ability to see another dimension of the creative challenges humanity faces in the world today, which may enhance our chances of transforming the creative challenges into creative opportunities.

References

Alexander, C. (2002). *The nature of order: An essay on the art of building and the nature of the universe: Book One: The phenomenon of life*. Berkeley, CA: Center for Environmental Structure.

Allen, P. (1995). *Art is a way of knowing: A guide to self-knowledge and spiritual fulfillment through creativity*. Boston: Shambhala.

Bodaken, B., & Fritz, R. (2006). *The managerial moment of truth: The essential step in helping people improve performance*. New York: Free Press.

Bogart, A. (2001). *A director prepares: Seven essays on art and science*. New York: Routledge.

Bogart, A. (2007). *And then, you act: Making art in an unpredictable world*. New York: Routledge.

Csikszentmihalyi, M. (1996). *Creativity: Flow and the psychology of discovery and invention*. New York: HarperCollins.

Csikszentmihalyi, M. (1997). *Finding flow: The psychology of engagement with everyday life*. New York: HarperCollins.

Glaser, B. G., & Strauss, A. L. (1965). *The awareness of dying*. Chicago: Aldine.

Glaser, B. G., & Strauss, A. L. (1967). *The discovery of grounded theory: Strategies for qualitative research*. Chicago: Aldine.

Hawkes, J. (2004). *The fourth pillar of sustainability: Culture's essential role in public planning*. Altona, AUS: Common Ground.

Henri, R. (1923, 1951). *The art spirit*. New York: Westview, HarperCollins.

Hubbard, B. M. (1998). *Conscious evolution: Awakening the power of our social potential*. Novato, CA: New World Library.

Jaworski, J. (1998). *Synchronicity: The inner path of leadership*. San Francisco: Berrett-Koehler.

Kaiser, M. (2009). Talk on *Arts in Crisis: A Kennedy Center Initiative*. Seattle: Benaroya Hall.

Kaupelis, R. (1980). *Experimental drawing*. New York: Watson-Guptill.

Kotter, J. (2005). *Our iceberg is melting: Changing and succeeding under any conditions*. New York: St. Martin's Press.

Kouzes, J., & Posner, B. (2002). *The leadership challenge* (3rd ed.). San Francisco: Jossey-Bass.

Maslow, A. (1970). *Religion, values and peak experiences*. New York: Viking.

Matanovic, M. (1985). *Lightworks: Explorations in art, culture, and creativity*. Issaquah, WA: Lorian.

McNiff, S. (1998a). *Art-based research*. Philadelphia: Jessica Kingsley.

McNiff, S. (1998b). *Trust the process: An artist's guide to letting-go*. Boston: Shambhala.

Moyers, B. (1999). *Fooling with words: A celebration of poets and their craft*. New York: William Morrow.

Mumford, L. (1956). *The transformations of man*. New York: Harper & Brothers.

Parks, S. D. (2005). *Leadership can be taught: A bold approach for a complex world*. Boston: Harvard Business School Press.

Pogrebin, R. (2009, June 4). Obama names republican to lead the humanities endowment. *The New York Times*, p. C1.

Ray, M. (1999). Social creativity as an heroic path in world crisis. In R. Purser & A. Montuori (Eds.), *Social creativity* (Vol. II, pp. 293–312). Cresskill, NJ: Hampton Press.

Roditi, E. (1980). *Dialogues on art*. Santa Barbara: Ross-Erikson.

Sawyer, K. (2007). *Group genius: The creative power of collaboration*. New York: Basic Books.

Senge, P. (2007). Foreword. In O. Scharmer, *Theory U: Leading from the future as it emerges* (pp. vii–xiv). Cambridge, MA: Society for Organizational Learning.

Strauss, A., & Corbin, J. (1990). *Basics of qualitative research: Grounded theory procedures and techniques*. Thousand Oaks: Sage.

Wheatley, M. (2005). *Finding our way: Leadership for an uncertain time*. San Francisco: Berrett-Koehler.

World Commission on Culture and Development. (1995). *Our creative diversity*. Retrieved from www.unesco.org/culture_and_development/ocd/intro.html

Using Critical Pedagogy to Critique Power Issues in Transformational Leadership

Laura M. Harrison

My experiences in teaching courses in organizational theory and leadership contrast sharply. In organizational theory, we take a trip that generally starts in the Industrial Revolution and ends in the current millennium, with Margaret Wheatley (2006) dissecting the large bureaucracies that failed the victims of Hurricane Katrina. We deduce that the complexities of contemporary society require systems thinking to affect substantive change and that small, decentralized networks of ordinary citizens were the organizations that responded most effectively after the storm. A substantial body of literature illuminating both the theoretical and practical aspects of systems thinking aids us in drawing these conclusions. I have yet to hear a student complain, "This is too pie in the sky," or "This is okay for the classroom, but totally unrealistic for actual life." Discussions tend to go well, with students offering practical application of systems theory to problems they encounter in their organizations. I offer this description as a contrast to my experience teaching leadership courses.

Leadership tends to start off well as we tour through the "Great Man" theories and work our way toward transformational leadership, but once we arrive, things get dicey. Students start looking at the clock, opening laptops for purposes other than taking notes, and otherwise generally checking out. When I mention the energy loss in the room, the "pie in the sky" comments emerge. The braver students share the sentiment that Martin Luther King Jr. and Mohandas Gandhi are inspirational but are inaccessible as models. Some students articulate a disconnect with transformational leadership theory, stating that it is simply neither relevant nor realistic for the kinds of organizational conundrums they face in their daily lives. I resisted these ideas initially, but the students' comments ultimately illuminated why I found transformational leadership so difficult to teach.

The Vision Problem

When I confront a pedagogical challenge, I try to reflect on my experience as a student learning similar material. I must admit I reacted identically to my students during classes in my own doctoral program when transformational leadership was the topic. Professors and authors emphasized the role of vision frequently, discussing it in general terms with broad applications in contexts ranging from business to politics to religion. The expression "There's no there there" often came to mind as I read the texts and listened to the lectures, both of which left me feeling that transformational leadership was essentially about having and selling a vision. Tierney (1989) defined the problem as follows: "The other authors either drop the concern for morality entirely from their discussion, or they translate moral action into the ability to create a 'vision.' In doing so, individuals such as Lee Iacocca or Fredrick Taylor gain the same credence as a Gandhi or a King. One wonders upon what basis anyone can claim that Iacocca had the moral interests of his followers in mind when he downsized the workforce by 60,000 employees" (p.164). Tierney's words articulated a key challenge in both teaching and learning transformational leadership theory: namely, there is no shared understanding of what transformational leadership seeks to transform. If transformational leadership applies to both the leader of the civil rights movement and a corporate tycoon, then one could argue that convincing people to adopt her or his vision makes a person a transformational leader whether that vision is for racial equality or selling more cars. In other words, if transformational leadership is about everything, then it's about nothing.

While secondary sources on transformational leadership obscure the ethical dimension of vision as Tierney (1989) described, primary sources speak to a clear moral imperative. Burns's (1978) seminal work, *Leadership*, defined transformational leadership as something that "becomes moral in that it raises the level of human conduct and ethical aspiration of both leader and led, and thus has a transforming effect on both" (p. 20). Indeed, discussions of transformational leadership frequently evoke Martin Luther King and Mohandas Gandhi, suggesting a strong social justice component to the kind of vision it seeks to extend. But this progressive impulse is shaky at best, given the lack of consensus about the extent to which transformational leadership requires a commitment to social change (Kezar, 2006). This inconsistency reveals one of the more interesting features of transformational leadership for both students and teachers: namely, its ambivalence about the role of power in developing and promoting a vision.

Those who teach and study transformational leadership have good reasons not to be more explicit about its radical possibilities. Sinclair (2007) captured this phenomenon deftly in her critical reflection on teaching leadership with an emphasis on dominance and subordination in organizations. Sinclair wrote of the corporate sponsors funding the students as people understandably invested in a "conventional educational product," not a critique of traditional management practices (p. 468). Sinclair's experience suggests the source for transformational leadership's hesitance when power analyses are concerned; it is politically untenable to teach students to question the system they seek to join through participation in your class.

For this political reason, discussions of transformational leadership often dodge issues of power and privilege. Much is written about the qualities that make individual transformational leaders successful in imparting the neutral vision Tierney (1989) described. However, few scholars focused on transformational leadership have produced work that focuses on the structural inequalities of the system that is to be transformed. (The emerging field of critical management studies provides a notable exception.) Fletcher warned of those with a vested interest in the status quo appropriating the aspects of transformational leadership envisioned by revolutionaries like Martin Luther King and Mohandas Gandhi: "The transformational promise of postheroic leadership (i.e., transformational leadership) is in danger of being co-opted. New models of leadership that are rooted in a different, more relational and interdependent belief system—or logic of effectiveness—about what leads to business success cannot flourish in structures and systems organized around beliefs in individualistic meritocracy" (2004, p. 658).

Until the system under consideration for transformation is the clear subject of inquiry, the qualities of individual transformational leaders are of little interest because they lack the necessary context for determining the "there there." Put another way, it is one thing to admire Martin Luther King Jr. and Mohandas Gandhi as individual transformational leaders safely tucked in the annals of history; it is another thing to drill down into the contemporary systems of white supremacy and colonialism each man fought. As Fletcher argued, it is necessary to understand the ways in which power operates at the deepest level of assumption in an organizational system in order to do the work it takes to first unmask it, then name it, then change it. Otherwise transformational leadership efforts are unlikely to be sustainable because the root power issues remain unaddressed.

For me, the first step in the process of considering transformational leadership's emancipatory potential was to understand deeply the impossibility of a power-neutral vision. It was not until one of the last classes in my doctoral program, when I came across Giroux's (1993) Border Crossings, that I gained the language I needed to convey more broadly the problem Tierney (1989) described regarding the vision issue in transformational leadership. Tierney notes, "Visions always belong to someone, and to the degree that they translate into curricula and pedagogical practices, they not only denote a struggle over forms of political authority and orders of representation, but also weigh heavily in regulating the moral identities, collective voices, and futures of others" (p. 92). Giroux's words and the class where I learned them (Critical Pedagogy and Participatory Research) helped me see how ideology disguised as objective rationality functioned to obfuscate power's role in the idea of vision undergirding transformational leadership theory. I gained a lexicon for interrogating systemic power, understanding Zinn's (2002) assertion and book title, "You can't be neutral on a moving train." This new and provocative material excited me as a student, offering me a framework for understanding systemic power in my lived experience in organizations.

As I progressed through school and began teaching, I integrated critical pedagogy into my understanding of transformational leadership. I no longer felt there was "no there there" in transformational leadership; in fact, I could see the relationship between its theoretical orientation toward social change and critical pedagogy's conceptual framework for interrogating systemic power. While I found these connections intellectually stimulating, teaching transformational leadership within a critical pedagogy lens stretched both my students and me in ways I had not anticipated. More specifically, I had to carefully consider student expectations of what education means in light of their fifteen-plus years in learning arrangements almost exclusively characterized by what Freire (1993) called the "banking concept" of school. The banking concept refers to conventional classroom practices wherein teachers deposit knowledge into students' heads. Many students appreciate a different approach once this traditional practice is articulated as expression of ideology, not any sort of objective reality about how classrooms should operate. Coming to this awareness must be understood as a process, however, and this is where I realized I had to examine my own assumptions about what it means to shift one's pedagogical practices from teacher centered to student centered.

Transformational Leadership in Transactional Classrooms

While there are many points of view about what transformational leadership is, there is general agreement about what it is *not*: transactional leadership. Some scholars argue that transformational and transactional forms of leadership are not mutually exclusive (for example, Mangham & Pye, 1991), but leadership textbooks almost universally position the transactional model as a foil for transformational leadership, such as in the following excerpt from Northouse's (2004) popular *Leadership Theory and Practice* text: "Transactional leadership refers to the bulk of leadership models, which focus on the exchanges that occur between leaders and their followers. Politicians who win votes by promising no new taxes are demonstrating transactional leadership. . . . In contrast to transactional leadership, transformational leadership refers to the process whereby an individual engaged with others and creates a connection . . . " (p. 170). Defining transformational leadership against that which is transactional raises a pedagogical challenge, since traditional classrooms epitomize transactional spaces. For example, instructors design the syllabus and establish the parameters in which students must perform to receive a grade, thus leading the class in much the way Northouse described as classic transactional leadership. Students experience incongruence between transformational leadership theory and transactional classrooms, a phenomenon that critical pedagogy can mitigate to some extent.

Critical pedagogy argues for reimagining the taken-for-granted features of conventional schooling (for example, teacher-centered syllabus, one-way knowledge transmission) as defaults that create the classroom as a politicized space (McKenna, 2003). While traditionalists argue these defaults are universal and there-

fore politically neutral, critical pedagogy exposes them as structural enforcements that perpetuate dominant class interests
(McLaren, 2003). The literature provides guideposts for ways
instructors can use critical pedagogy to teach transformational
leadership, thus modeling an alternative to the transactional
processes that characterize the traditional classroom. Examples
include problem-posing dialogue (Freire, 1993), case-in-point
teaching (Parks, 2005), and foregrounding group process (Hay &
Hodgkinson, 2006).

The aforementioned examples provide excellent practices for
disrupting the transactional, teacher-centered classroom dynamic. While some students embrace these techniques as a
welcome change, others find the experience confusing or frus-
trating. Much of the critical pedagogy literature, including Freire
(1993), Parks (2005), and Hay and Hodgkinson (2006), reference student struggle when a class fails to conform to their
assumptions about what class should look like. In her critical
reflection about using critical pedagogy to teach MBA students,
Sinclair (2007) wrote that students went as far as to question the
legitimacy of the class as well as her expertise as the instructor.

These challenges of using critical pedagogy in a traditional
educational system mirrored my own experience as a new instructor trying to force my students to unlearn more than a decade
of education based on the banking philosophy only to demand
their conformity to my expectations. My first round of evaluations reflected the fact that I was not reaching my students by
exposing them too quickly to an experience that is inherently
disequilibriating. If I wanted them to tolerate me causing them
discomfort by disrupting their taken-for-granted assumptions
about what constitutes legitimate knowledge, then I had to listen
to what was important to them and frame the material within
that context. I started e-mailing them before the first class session,
asking them to tell me what confounds them most about leadership and/or organizational politics based on their experience in
the workforce. Once I had this data, I could craft course content

that was truly student centered, using their responses to contextualize some of the more unfamiliar material. I also learned to begin the class fairly close to their expectation of what a legitimate professor looks like, slowly turning it over to them as I gained the credibility needed to entice them to experiment with less transactional, more transformational ways of learning.

Ultimately, I found critical pedagogy helpful in creating a classroom space that was less transactional and more likely to model the power critique I wanted to highlight in transformational leadership. I could demonstrate how one might disrupt practices that serve the status quo, but I learned quickly that I needed to both show and tell very specifically about how power works before I could begin to teach how transformational leaders affect change. As Dehler, Welsh, and Lewis explained, "When creating alternative understandings by illuminating power considerations, wading into the grayness of pedagogical borders and problematizing the organizational context, content that is produced and legitimated so readily in traditional textbooks now becomes more complex" (2001, p. 505). Addressing this complexity required equipping students with an intellectual toolkit of sorts so that they had the language they needed to question their underlying assumptions in the classroom and beyond. I could speak of concepts like hegemony, ideology, master narrative, and counter-narrative, but I needed an example to make these terms more tangible.

Martin Luther King Jr. and Mohandas Gandhi are visible as individuals, but the power structures they confronted are more difficult to investigate. Systemic power is difficult to surface precisely because the interests of the powerful are masked as objective reality. Ironically, interrogating a system seemed to require creating an artificial organization in which students could gain the distance they needed to observe power dynamics as outsiders. Philip Zimbardo's legendary work on the Stanford Prison Experiment provides a useful case because it takes as its central question this idea of systemic power, demonstrating experimentally how normal individuals will oppress their classmates under the right organizational system. His research put a large dent in the essentialized notion of individual agency by showing how most healthy, sane individuals will either commit or stand by while others oppress their peers. "My appreciation of the power residing in systems started with an awareness of how institutions create mechanisms that translate ideology into operating procedures. In other words, my focus has widened considerably through a fuller appreciation of the ways in which situational conditions are created and shaped by higher order factors—systems of power. Systems, not just dispositions and situations, must be taken into account in order to understand complex behavior patterns" (Zimbardo, 2007, pp. 9–10). Based on his original experiment as well as his work since, Zimbardo asserts that hegemonic systems impede a person's ability to act in accordance with his or her individual values. Zimbardo did not state that it is impossible for a person to practice transformational leadership in a compromised system; in fact, he cited several examples of individuals standing up to tyrannical regimes, including the brave people who blew the whistle on the Abu Ghraib prison scandal in 2004. The argument Zimbardo does make is that there is significant power in organizational systems, and those who challenge it face potential consequences. This is an important understanding for those seeking to engage transformational leadership within organizations; simply having the right idea or the better vision is rarely enough if the policy one advocates runs counter to the institution's prevailing ideology.

When using the Stanford Prison Experiment to teach ideology as a conceptual tool, I am careful to emphasize that ideology is rarely stated. I use the Stanford Prison Experiment as a teaching device precisely because it provides a rare glimpse into the process of ideological formation made possible only under experimental condition. As a result, students witness another critical pedagogy concept: that is, the creation of a master narrative. The master narrative serves as a vehicle for reinforcing the paradigm of the status quo by providing a framework for understanding reality in a way that is biased toward those in power. In the Stanford Prison Experiment, students can see the creation of the master narrative in action as the guards construct stories about both themselves and the prisoners to justify the exploitation. Students gain a deeper appreciation for the few guards and prisoners who created a counter-narrative based on their ability to reveal the master narrative as the ideology of the dominant, not objective reality. In the process, they develop a fuller understanding of what transformational leadership truly demands.

Making Transformational Leadership Possible for Students

Once I began using critical pedagogy to teach conceptual tools for analyzing power, students' reaction to transformational leadership shifted from bored to uneasy. They understood now that transformational leadership asked much more of them than coming up with a convincing vision and getting people to follow it. Complexifying transformational leadership as Dehler and colleagues (2001) described created a classroom space marked by some degree of anxiety, but also energy. What would it mean for them to construct counter-narratives to the company line in their organizations? Would they be asked to take stands that might compromise their ability to get ahead in their companies? Suddenly, the "real-world" implications of transformational leadership felt tangible to students. The pedagogical challenge at this point was to channel their discomfort into critical examination of what Parks (2005) called "swamp issues," the messy everyday business in organizations.

In my experience, figures like Martin Luther King Jr. and Gandhi offer useful examples of transformational leadership's social justice prerogative but can mislead students into dichotomous thinking about change. The discourse on these figures creates the impression that organizational change is either accomplished by a lone crusader taking on an evil institution or that it is not even possible, in the "You can't fight city hall" sense. Badaracco (2002) presented an alternative vision, postulating "quiet leaders" who affect change by gaining and maintaining access to the table where the day-to-day decisions get made. He notes, "Sustained leadership usually means becoming an insider. This gives leaders the opportunity to use power and influence responsibly, on many issues and over extended periods. But people don't become insiders by accident. They must look out for themselves, protect their positions, and stay at the table so they can continue to lead. In other words, they need to have a healthy sense of self-regard" (Badaracco, 2002, p. 35). This tension between gaining access to power as an insider while challenging the system as an outsider excited students because it captured their fears about self-preservation. As Badaracco suggested, there is a finite number of times a person can take an absolute stand against an organizational policy or procedure without losing the very position from which he or she could affect positive change. This idea resonates with students, who understandably fear the risks of confronting powerful interests in their own organizations.

Part of the strategy for enacting the social justice vision in transformational leadership must come from rethinking the position of individuals inside and outside of organizations. Organizations are paradoxically misunderstood as either benignly rational and therefore not in need of change or as all powerful and therefore not changeable. Individuals, then, are stuck with the choice of following orders or putting their necks on the line, very possibly to be cut given the conservative nature of organizations concerning change. In her work on organizational change, Meyerson (2003) advocated a third choice, coining the term *tempered radical* to describe the sort of person in an organization who straddles this insider-outsider divide. As she explained, "Tempered radicals are people who operate on a fault line. They are organizational insiders who contribute and succeed in their jobs. At the same time, they are treated as outsiders because they represent ideals or agendas that are somehow at odds with the dominant culture" (p. 5).

Meyerson blurred the line between organizational insider and outsider, providing a much-needed vision of where most students must function if they are to be effective in their organizations. By recognizing and acknowledging the power issues inherent in organizations, Meyerson offered a conceptual strategy for negotiating the complexity of political realities within institutional structures.

Helping students navigate power conundrums in their organizations seems to be an integral part of teaching transformational leadership theory. When possible, I prefer to offer strategies that are explicit, creative, and honest about the institutional situations in which potential change agents find themselves. The following description of what Shor termed "deviance credits" provides an example of such a strategy. "Another political method that helps is called 'deviance credits.' I think of this as taking on some of the harmless tasks of the institution so that you get recognized as a legitimate part of the scenery . . . If you take part in a variety of small tasks, you begin to slowly root yourself in the life of the institution. The recognition you get for doing this is like an account of credits that allows you more room to deviate" (Shor & Freire, 2003, p. 490). One quality that makes the deviance credit idea useful to students is the specific organizational context—in this case, institutions of higher education—as a reference point. Vaguely proclaiming that students need to embody social justice principles in their transformational leadership efforts connotes what Badaracco called "inspirational ethics literature" (1997, p. 5). As Badaracco asserts, this kind of proselytizing rarely helps people act as socially conscious transformational leaders in the milieu of everyday organizational life. Students need tools that shift the emphasis from an almost obsessive focus on individual leaders to the systems of power themselves as loci for transformational leadership.

Conclusion

There are two transformational leaderships. One skirts power issues and substitutes vague ideas about vision for Burns's (1978) original impulse toward moral action. I find it almost impossible to teach this version, because students catch on quickly that "there's no there there" and display what the critical pedagogy literature refers to as resistance; that is, "student oppositional behavior associated with their need to struggle against elements of dehumanization" (Darder, Baltodano, & Torres, 2003, p. 14). It would be unlikely for students to articulate their resistance oppositionally at the beginning of the class, but once they have the language to unpack hegemony both in and out of the classroom, they start asking questions like "Who benefits?" from textbooks and lectures lacking a power critique.

Transformational leadership offers exciting opportunities when we give students the intellectual tools they need to interrogate systems in such a way that opens possibilities for affecting change. Teaching that Martin Luther King Jr. and Mohandas Gandhi exemplify transformational leadership is not enough; students need to know exactly what these leaders did and how they did it. Without conceptual frameworks like ideology, hegemony, master narrative, and counter-narrative, students are left with a vague impression of these leaders as skilled orators who could inspire followership. Once students have the language they need to analyze structural power, however, they grasp the real genius of King and Gandhi. Students understand these transformational leaders as people who unmasked the conventional wisdom of their time, exposing it not as benignly rational but as white supremacist and creating the counter-narrative necessary for people to imagine and create an alternative.

Strategies for affecting change must accompany this understanding of transformational leadership as power critique or students may dismiss transformation as too unrealistic or daunting. Badaracco's (2002) quiet leader, Meyerson's (2003) tempered radical, and Shor and Freire's (2003) deviance credits present theoretical tools based on a realistic appraisal of systemic power. These three constructs offer students strategies that acknowledge the real challenges confronting those who seek to embody the revolutionary spirit of the transformer. Transformational leadership requires a delicate calculus of commitment to social justice, political savvy, and self-preservation, three topics with unlimited capacity to engage both students and teachers.

References

Badaracco, J. L., Jr. (1997). *Defining moments: When managers must choose between right and right.* Boston: Harvard Business School Press.

Badaracco, J. L., Jr. (2002). *Leading quietly: An unorthodox guide to doing the right thing.* Boston: Harvard Business School Press.

Burns, J. M. (1978). *Leadership.* New York: Harper & Row.

Darder, A., Baltodano, M., & Torres, R. (2003). *The critical pedagogy reader.* New York: RoutledgeFalmer.

Dehler, G., Welsh, M., & Lewis, M. (2001). Critical pedagogy in the "new paradigm." *Management Learning, 32*(4), 493–511.

Fletcher, J. (2004). The paradox of postheroic leadership: An essay on gender, power, and transformational change. *The Leadership Quarterly, 15,* 647–661.

Freire, P. (1993). *Pedagogy of the oppressed.* New York: Continuum International.

Giroux, H. (1993). *Border crossings: Cultural workers and the politics of education.* New York: Routledge.

Hay, A., & Hodgkinson, M. (2006). Rethinking leadership: A way forward for teaching leadership? *Leadership & Organization Development Journal, 27,* 144–158.

Kezar, A. (2006). Rethinking the L-word in higher education. *ASHE Higher Education Report, 31*(6).

Mangham, I., & Pye, A. (1991). *The doing of managing.* Oxford: Blackwell.

McKenna, T. (2003). Borderness and pedagogy: Exposing culture in the classroom. In A. Darder, M. Baltodano, & R. Torres (Eds.), *The critical pedagogy reader* (pp. 430–439). New York: RoutledgeFalmer.

McLaren, P. (2003). Critical pedagogy: A look at the major concepts. In A. Darder, M. Baltodano, & R. Torres (Eds.), *The critical pedagogy reader* (pp. 69–95). New York: RoutledgeFalmer.

Meyerson, D. (2003). *Tempered radicals: How everyday leaders inspire change at work.* Boston: Harvard Business School Press.

Northouse, P. (2004). *Leadership theory and practice.* Thousand Oaks, CA: Sage.

Parks, S. D. (2005). *Leadership can be taught: A bold approach for a complex world.* Boston: Harvard Business School Press.

Shor, I., & Freire, P. (2003). What are the fears and risks of transformation? In A. Darder, M. Baltodano, & R. Torres (Eds.), *The critical pedagogy reader* (pp. 479–498). New York: RoutledgeFalmer.

Sinclair, A. (2007). Teaching leadership critically to MBAs: Experiences from heaven and hell. *Management Learning, 38*(4), 458–472.

Tierney, W. (1989). Advancing democracy: A critical interpretation of leadership. *Peabody Journal of Education, 66*(3), 157–175.

Wheatley, M. (2006). *Leadership and the new science: Discovering order in a chaotic world.* San Francisco: Berrett-Koehler.

Zimbardo, P. (2007). *The Lucifer effect: Understanding how good people turn evil.* New York: Random House.

Zinn, H. (2002). *You can't be neutral on a moving train.* Boston: Beacon Press.

Teaching Leadership for Socially Just Schools

A Transformational Approach

Michael I. Poutiatine and
Dennis Arthur Conners

Current accountability policies in schools create challenges that are issues of equity and justice. Such conditions test school leaders who want to transcend and transform traditional practices in public education. Recent research, however, raises concerns about the quality of educational leadership preparation and the professional learning needed for socially just leadership (Gerzon, 2006; Levine, 2005; Terrell & Lindsey, 2008). In a systematic review across schools of education leadership preparation programs, Levine (2005) concludes, "Their curricula are disconnected from the needs of the leaders in schools. Their admission standards are among the lowest in American graduate schools. Their professorate is ill equipped to educate school leaders" (p. 24).

Levine (2005) and others (Hargreaves, Earl, Moore & Manning, 2000; Intrator & Kunzman, 2006) call for a radically new leadership philosophy and for preparation beyond the "traditional" models often found in higher education. If we are to transform our schools into more effective places to educate *all* students for the twenty-first century, we must prepare transformative school leaders who ground their leadership in the moral imperatives necessary for socially just practice.

Through this kind of leadership, we activate the capacity for vibrant learning, best practices, and the deeper pursuit of socially just schools (Marshall & Olivia, 2006). The call, therefore, as we hear it, is for an integrated program approach that connects transformative learning theories with leadership practice, the academy in partnership with schools, the prospective leadership practitioner with authentic practice, and perhaps most important, the *skill* required for effective and moral school leadership with the *will* required for effective and socially just leadership (Lindsey, Nuri Robins, & Terrell, 2003; Michelli & Keiser, 2005). In this chapter, we frame the theoretical implications of teaching leadership skill and apply that theoretical base to a practiced model for preparing school leaders who live and practice social justice.

Schools and Social Justice

Definitions of social justice abound (Bogotch, 2002; Connell, 1993; Marshall & Ward, 2004). Numerous scholars' definitions involve equity and marginalization (Gewirtz, 1998; Goldfarb & Grinberg, 2002). We build on their definitions and incorporate Bogotch's (2002) assertion that "there are no fixed or predictable meanings of social justice prior to actually engaging in educational leadership practices" (p. 153). The connection between leadership and social justice is defined not in universal terms, but in the realities of public school work; thus, we use Theoharis's (2004) definition of leadership for social justice: administrators "advocate, lead and keep at the center of their practice and vision issues of race, class, gender, language, disability, sexual orientation, and other historically marginalizing factors" (p. 8).

To make social justice connections in all details and interactions, school leaders require not only the lenses that offer a vision of a socially just school (and the will to wear them), but also the skill to see that vision as an integral part of each decision. Social justice requires, for example, keeping issues of marginalization at the center of everything from scheduling to staffing.

A Paradox: Skill and Will

For most leaders, practicing socially just leadership requires fundamental shifts in how we think about both leadership and ourselves as leaders. The usual technical questions of leadership—the *what* and the *how*—are important, but we must likewise pay attention to the essential questions: the *why* and the *who* (Palmer, 1998a). As Palmer describes, the essence of our leadership is, "We [lead] who we are" (p. 2). How do we define who we are? For Palmer, "Human beings were made for relationships" (p. 65). Herein lies the paradox inherent in school leadership: Socially just leadership manifests at base from the individual leader, but it is also profoundly manifest through relationships in community. So which is more important: the leader or the community? The answer is yes.

The Leader

"Self" as the core of leadership is a common understanding for many who study and teach leadership (Bennis, 2003; Bolman & Deal, 2001; Kouzes & Posner, 2003b; Maxwell, 1993). But so much of this work generally amounts to "Know thyself" and "Improve thyself." Knowing and improving are not enough for socially just practice in schools. Palmer notes, "Good [leadership] cannot be reduced to technique; good [leadership] comes from the identity and integrity of the [leader]" (1998a, p. 10). The *internal* identity and integrity of the leader are crucial, for if a leader fails to offer true selfhood in any relationship, all that can be offered (externally) is pretense. Scharmer claims that "the success of any [leadership] depends on the *interior condition* of the [leader], so it is not only what leaders do and how they do it, but their interior condition" that matters (2007, p. 27; emphasis added). Without integrity, connection between internal self and external relationship, any relationship becomes meaningless. Without authenticity, we become caricatures of ourselves. Thus, to embody a leadership approach that is grounded in social justice, leaders must be able to connect who they are with what they do.

To develop leaders with this capacity, we must provide developmental and transformational experiences that impel leaders into exploring their inner-life understandings at the same time that they learn the skill capacities to act in educational systems. We must simultaneously develop leadership *skill* (knowledge and capacity) and leadership *will* (the grounded connection with identity and integrity).

Developing Leadership Presence: Skill and Will

Hundreds of books offer models for the development of leadership skills (Bass, 2008). Generally these books associate specific leadership theories with practice and include ideas like those of relational leadership (Kouzes & Posner, 2002), leadership communication (Hackman & Johnson, 2000), authority (Heifetz, Grashow, & Linksy, 2009), credibility (Kouzes & Posner, 2003a), task and process management (Yukl, 2006), and so on. There are also many excellent pedagogical and developmental models for the building of leadership skill capacities; leadership simulation, case study, and behavior modeling have all proven effective (Bass, 2008, pp. 1071–1086). These skills are essential to effective leadership and must be part of any leadership development process, but they are by no means sufficient to the development of socially just leaders.

Development of Leadership Will

In the context of leadership development, *will* means understanding and asserting an inherent power of choice in the world. It is what Palmer calls our ability to choose to shed our light or darkness on the world (1998b) as we co-create a communal vision. Will is an idealized concept in this context; that is, will calls us to want to make choices for a better world. While the power of choice may be innate, in order to understand and assert that choice ethically, the leader must have a reference or guide, much like an internal compass (Korthagen & Vasalos, 2008) that exists at the core of our being. Leadership will must be founded internally, in identity, core values, and mission (Korthagen & Vasalos, 2005). We believe that leadership skill can be developed through learning and practice, but leadership will must be brought forth from within to direct skill and practice.

A connection with, and awareness of, core identity allows leaders to exercise leadership will with integrity. That connection and awareness comes only through a deep understanding of the self-referential question, "Who is it that leads?" This question reveals the difference between leadership will and integrity: Whereas integrity generally refers to the connection between who a leader is and what that leader does (action) (Kouzes & Posner, 2002), will speaks to the deep roots of being that make integrity possible (belief). *Acting* with leadership integrity requires that our actions and our beliefs be aligned. Leadership will, then, is the self-awareness of the connection between leadership and being and the willingness or desire to act with integrity. Without a deep and intentional leadership will, relationships are only skin deep. How, then, can we develop a leadership will that will enable school leaders to connect in relationships of integrity?

Learning to Lead for Social Justice

We believe the field of leadership studies lacks the language to speak articulately about both skill and will development for school leaders. To begin to articulate an integrated approach honoring both skill and will, we borrow existing language from other disciplines. Formational education (Foster, Dahill, Golemon, & Tolentino, 2006) offers useful ways to talk about the development of leadership will that can complement the established language of leadership skill development.

Foster and colleagues (2006) define *formational education* as "a process by which the student *becomes* a certain kind of thinking, feeling and acting being" (emphasis added, p. 10). Formational learning in this view is about the development of a deeper identity, what we call *leadership will*, that "originates in the deepest intentions for professional service" (p. 100) and "functions as a lens or framework though which [leaders] view and appropriate the knowledge and skill associated with the work" (p. 101). The adoption of formational pedagogies (Foster et al., 2006; Intrator & Kunzman, 2006; Korthagen, 2004; Palmer, 1998a, 2004; Scharmer, 2007; Thompson, 2000) can provide a map into a world of leadership will that enables a better connection of leadership skill with ethical leadership process. We should not forsake effective skill capacity pedagogies but should integrate a formational approach with existing pedagogies to foster skill *and* will development.

Integrating formational pedagogy (Foster et al., 2006) into leadership development curricula while supporting and augmenting effective traditional methods (Bass, 2008) creates a framework for leadership development that is more clearly grounded in the selfhood of the leaders and more directed toward socially just practices.

Leadership Formation for School Leaders

There are myriad ways to prepare school leaders for a more holistic and integrated practice. We present one model that has seen constructive effects and that has tremendous potential to educate and develop future leaders.

The Leadership Formation Program

From 1998 to 2008, Gonzaga University's Leadership Formation Program (LFP) took an innovative approach to preparing principals, program administrators, and superintendents through a nontraditional graduate certification program. Profound lessons arose from the design of the program, which focused on the preparation of school leaders committed to transforming themselves and schools in a socially just manner.

LFP Structure: The Virtual School District. The curriculum of the LFP was organized using a "problem posing" (Freire, 1970), extended case study approach built on the idea of active learning. Addressing real-life problems presented a significant alternative to studying blocks of classified knowledge in a strictly organized sequence. To that end, a Web-based virtual school district was created as a real-time learning lab for leadership candidates. The fictitious Mountain Lakes School District, in the virtual state of Columbia, served as the "first job" for candidates admitted to the program. A five-member faculty team comprised of the university-based program director, one practicing superintendent, one central office administrator, and two principals designed the case study, delivered instruction, and assessed candidates.

Pedagogical Design. The imperative to teach leadership for transformation and social justice encouraged faculty to press candidates beyond ordinary cognitive exercises. Too often graduate students are exposed to and espouse a commitment to social justice but lack the opportunity to test their beliefs until they are responsible for real schools and real students. The use of a complex case scenario alongside provocative seminars and the intentional practice of a particular set of skill capacities pushed candidates to grapple with the challenges posed to educational leaders in today's world. This integration of cognitive learning and affective practice was accomplished through three main pedagogical components.

Seminars. Candidates themselves were responsible for leading LFP seminars on the cohort's required readings. These readings, by hooks (1994), Freire (1970), Postman (1996), Hirsch (1999), and others, were selected with questions of social justice in education in mind. The experience of preparing for and leading a seminar developed a capacity in candidates to pose thoughtful questions and to create a space in which true dialogue (Bohm, 1996) could occur.

Critical Skill Capacities. A second pedagogical element in the LFP was the mastery of "leadership disciplines" found in Senge's *The Fifth Discipline* (1990). An assumption of this program was that true school leaders hold strong beliefs and can achieve results in the service of those beliefs at the same time that they remain open to learning. Senge's five leadership disciplines encompassing five major skill capacities (personal mastery, mental models, shared vision, team learning, and systems thinking) encouraged candidates to acquire characteristics necessary for effective school leadership (pp. 68–73).

Simulations. Simultaneous to completing seminar readings and gaining skill competencies, every candidate in the LFP was placed in at least one individual and one group simulation as a practicing school administrator. Candidates not participating in a particular simulation served as critical observers. Each simulation was carefully constructed always to include both skill and will components; this combination proved to be the genius behind the simulation pedagogy. Simulations were created to address such issues of school leadership skill as budgeting, data collection and use, legal issues, curriculum and supervision, and so on. Simulations also addressed issues of leadership will by posing seemingly skill-based problems in terms that required the candidates to access their deepest values about education.

Simulation Example: Schools and Immigration

In most leadership contexts, as we know, it is rarely the technical leadership questions (Heifetz, 1994) that are the really difficult ones. Rather, the questions that arise from complex and ambiguous contexts, and that require the leader to examine deeply held beliefs about justice and selfhood, prove to be the hardest. A simulation example can demonstrate the pedagogical implications of examining such questions.

Contextual Overview. A novice principal arrives at school for his or her first hours of work on a hot summer day and meets a recently arrived, illegal immigrant Mexican mother who wants to register her children for school. The mother speaks only Spanish; the principal does not speak Spanish and hastily finds a translator.

Political Context. The virtual state of Columbia has recently passed a law that forbids the state to spend money to educate illegal immigrants. The virtual law was contested, but it stands as the law of the land. In the virtual School District of Mountain Lakes, the superintendent (an LFP candidate) has been required by the state's Office of Public Instruction to submit his or her district policy for compliance with this new law.

Policy Context. The Mountain Lakes School District administrative team has met and created a new policy, sent that morning to the novice principal (LFP candidate) by the superintendent, that requires verification of legal status for all students as well as the utilization of a new and intrusive registration form. The policy is effective immediately.

Simulation Preparation. The LFP candidate receives the "case" in advance and prepares for the simulation by anticipating issues and forecasting possible responses. This preparation includes the inner work of examining core values. Many candidates at this stage espouse theories of social justice without fully understanding how they will apply in a face-to-face meeting.

The actor playing the role of the Mexican parent places the initial issue before the new principal, but there is no script for what follows. The physical space for this simulation is carefully prepared by faculty to represent a real office. It offers a safe yet challenging arena for the candidate to practice skill capacities and to discern an identity as a leader in a complex context.

Simulation: Immigration. The principal begins by engaging the parent, but as the conversation unfolds through the interpreter, the principal falters as the mother entreats him or her. She explains that she has come here so that her children "can have a better life." She worries that she will be reported to the Immigration and Naturalization Service if she fills out the form, yet she knows that school is the only avenue by which her children can reach the life she envisions for them.

The principal immediately faces a question common to school leaders: What do I believe about education versus What does my job require of me? An intellectual exercise addressed through seminars, skill development, and self-reflection becomes a dunking in the messy reality of social injustice. The outcome of a complex simulation often reflects the internal clarity of the candidate's beliefs. Neither the principal candidate nor the observing cohort can escape the exercise without beginning to recognize their capacities to do harm in the service of their schools. Also inescapable is an understanding that espousing a belief in social justice is quite different from aligning action with that belief.

We believe the most difficult and challenging work of school leaders is discerning the answers to these questions: How do I lead from my beliefs in social justice when my job seems to require something else? How do I align my beliefs and my identity in school? Or, simply, What do I do when I don't know what to do?

Simulation Immigration: The Debrief. Following each simulation, faculty, actors, and all candidates in the observational circle participate in the debriefing. Observer candidates can query the principal and the parent, asking them to open up their thinking. The simulation becomes an arena of active inquiry and the creation of meaning. Candidate observers consistently recognized that it is one thing to observe and quite another to be "in the box." Confronting social injustice in human terms within the structured pedagogy of simulation is compelling in a way that neither reading about it nor watching can match.

The action that occurred within the simulation becomes part of the yearlong Mountain Lakes School District case. Initial debriefing can take several hours and is revisited at the next administrative team meeting as part of the real work of the virtual school district. Pedagogically, it is of equal importance to the simulation that candidates examine how thoroughly they understand the injustices they encounter and how deeply their encounter has affected their core values. To learn, they must wonder, What will I do as an educational leader when faced with injustice? The opportunity for reflection and change is the heart of the transformational nature of the program.

Leadership beyond Schools

Foster wrote that leadership, in whatever realm, is "differentiated from decision-making, from goal-setting, or from authority," because "it serves in a different way than the type of authority necessary to run an organization, build cars or accumulate real estate" (1989, p. 50). He argued that leadership needs to be seen as transcending management and that it must involve the critical, the transformative, the educative, and the ethical. Through examination of the design of the LFP, it becomes clear that the exercise of leadership, as presented to the candidates through their participation in simulations and throughout the program, was based on a set of assumptions that reflected Foster's ideals. The LFP steered clear of conventional wisdom about school leaders that aligns "school effectiveness" with managerial tasks. Rather, if school leaders can become visionary custodians who connect their own fully considered and deeply held beliefs about social justice and education to their actions with the real people who populate their schools, then schools can truly become places of transformative and ethical learning. The LFP brought the paradox of skill and will for school leaders to the forefront of the candidate's learning experience.

Leadership as Critical

The LFP conceived of human activity as essentially "constructed," passed down but reinterpreted and recreated in that passing. This approach is in contrast to a conception of activity as essentially received, passed down from generation to generation without much change. Construction casts the examination and critique of previous beliefs as one of the purposes of educational leadership in order to identify conditions of oppression and/or obstruction at play and to determine how to lessen oppression or obstruction. Candidates were encouraged to remember that they have agency, to see themselves as subjects in their learning, not simply as objects. Feeling their agency allows them to see that effective leadership is not strictly a cognitive exercise, but one that requires the identity of the leader to emerge. Failing to see themselves as having agency as school leaders may lead to their finding themselves in the service of fixed ideas or causes, and thus agents of static ideals or even injustice.

In the LFP, candidates learn that leadership at its heart is a critical practice, one that comments on constructions of reality, that holds up ideals for comparison, and that attempts to locate a current shared vision based on an interpretation of the past. In critical practice, then, leadership is oriented not just toward the development of more effective organizational structures, but more important, toward a transformation of life practices in which the ideals of freedom and democracy are foremost.

Leadership as Transformative

The critical spirit of leadership, as taught by the LFP, leads naturally to the notion of transformation. Leadership is and must be oriented toward social change. Burns's (2003) view of transformational leadership documents persons who evoked periods of progress and development that have transformed the course of human events. Gandhi is one example; Martin Luther King Jr. is another. These leaders effected transformation of consciousness, and, as a result, social and political transformation ensued.

Yet transformation is not found only in certain grand moments of history. Rather, it happens every day, when leaders who might consider themselves regular people exert positive influence. The LFP case study and simulation provide a crucible for learning this important point. Social change can be accomplished without the complete restructuring of any given society, just as meaningful educational change can occur without a complete restructuring of a school district. However, social change does require the integration of skill and will in leadership, toward a transformative vision.

Leadership as Educative

To the degree that leadership can critique traditions that are oppressive (Apple, 2000; Freire, 1970) and can aim for a transformation of such conditions, leadership must be educative. Analysis assumes that the leader enables self-reflection; in the LFP's virtual school district setting, analysis means devoting time to talk about the district's history and purpose as well as the distribution of power. Such reflection upon policy and procedural arrangements allows for a deep understanding of the district's restraints upon or promotion of human agency and social justice.

Providing a vision of ways in which the district's and the community's practices could be altered so that they meet constituents' needs while providing a sense of meaning is perhaps the most crucial role of leadership. Leaders must show new social arrangements while demonstrating continuity with the past; and they must show how new social structures connect to the basic mission, goals, and objectives of important relationships while creating a compelling vision of the future.

Leadership as Ethical

The final dimension of leadership as practiced in the LFP is its ethical commitment. First, individual ethical commitments were made by the soon-to-be leaders. Second were the overall commitments by the candidates in the program to envision themselves as part of an ethical community.

The first commitment is related to learning to reach the various objectives necessary to run the Mountain Lakes School District through the use of power. Candidates learned in real time that leadership involves power relationships and that these relationships can be used positively or negatively. The complexities of the simulation case studies offered candidates a hands-on feel for negative power relationships, such as those that would achieve the ends desired by the fictional state. This, in Burns's term, is "power wielding" (2003, p. 16). Most candidates concluded that power wielding is not leadership at all. Many came to understand that ethical leadership is founded on a moral relationship in which their actions and intentions work to elevate, not oppress. In the immigration simulation case, this aspect of moral relationship was exemplified as deeply understanding the relationship between the leader and the immigrant mother. Ethical leadership had the capacity to critique social conditions within the state, the school district, and the school that resulted in policies of exclusion and discrimination. Ethical leadership could offer new possibilities for those social arrangements for all district constituents and find productive ways in which the mother could make appropriate arrangements for the education of her children.

However, the ethical aspects of leadership in this instance extend further than the particular leaders' relationship with the immigrant mother and her needs. Rather, leadership in the way the LFP proposed it would be to recognize the ethical orientation the leader holds toward the entire Mountain Lakes community. Leaders have a twofold duty: first, to understand themselves, recognizing that their search for the "good life" is inextricably tied to a set of democratic values shared by many others; and second, to assist others in understanding and assisting in the various options for living that life, so that the leader's good life does not come at the expense of the good of the community.

Conclusion

During the debrief of our young principal in the LFP immigration simulation, the candidate felt a bit embarrassed by his performance. It wasn't that he felt he had not effectively run a meeting with a parent; he felt he had. He clearly understood and articulated the policies of his school and district, and he was thoroughly professional in his approach. He felt embarrassed because he did not know what to do when his core values came directly in conflict with his organizational policy mandate; because he did not have an answer to the question, "What do you do when you don't know what to do?"

Leaders face this question all the time. One of the faculty-tutors in the LFP program, a high school principal, explained, "I am doing things to kids now that I swore I would never do. In the name of standards and accountability and leave no child untested, I am doing damage to kids and teachers that I cannot even fathom—and it is tearing me up inside, every day." What the candidate in the simulation called "embarrassment," the experienced school leader identified as "tearing . . . up inside," each of them recognizing the disconnect between their internal values and the external requirements of the job. The principal continued, "Every day I go to work now and wonder what little compromise of my soul I will be required to make today. I wonder if it is all worth it; I wonder if I can do enough; I wonder if I am enough. . . . You know, they never taught me any of this in 'Principal School.' I wish thirty years ago someone would have told me about how to keep your soul in this business—really that is what it is all about, keeping my soul for the sake of kids." It is critical to teach school leaders the capacities and dispositions that allow them to navigate ambiguous contexts in the job of school leadership, and we see these capacities and dispositions as essential if we want more socially just schools. These require not only skills and knowledge but a clear grounding in the beliefs and identity of the leader. If the effectiveness of leadership is always predicated on the internal state of the leader, we must be able to address the internal state in a developmental way. The Leadership Formation Program seeks to do this by addressing both skill and will.

It is clear that leadership is basic to the development of schools and systems that serve our children in socially responsible ways. However, not just any leadership approach can meet the challenges presented by the state of schooling in our culture. There may have been a time when school leaders merely needed to be technically competent to lead, but that time is gone. School leaders of the twenty-first century must think, feel, and act with integrity if they are to build schools where social justice is the practice as well as the ideal.

References

Apple, M. (2000). *Official knowledge*. New York: Routledge.

Bass, B. (2008). *The Bass handbook of leadership*. New York: Free Press.

Bennis, W. (2003). *On becoming a leader*. New York: Basic Books.

Bogotch, I. (2002). Educational leadership and social justice: Practice into theory. *Journal of School Leadership, 12*(2), 138–156.

Bohm, D. (1996). *On dialogue*. New York: Routledge.

Bolman, L., & Deal, T. (2001). *Leading with soul*. San Francisco: Jossey-Bass.

Burns, J. M. (2003). *Transforming leadership: A new pursuit of happiness*. New York: Grove.

Connell, R. (1993). *Schools and social justice.* Philadelphia: Temple University Press.

Foster, C., Dahill, L., Golemon, L. A., & Tolentino, B. (2006). *Educating clergy.* San Francisco: Jossey-Bass.

Foster, W. (1989). Toward a critical practice of leadership. In J. Smyth (Ed.), *Critical perspectives on educational leadership* (pp. 39–62). New York: RoutledgeFalmer.

Freire, P. (1970). *Pedagogy of the oppressed.* New York: Continuum.

Gerzon, M. (2006). *Leading through conflict.* Boston: Harvard Business School Press.

Gewirtz, S. (1998). Conceptualizing social justice in education: Mapping the territory. *Journal of Education Policy, 13*(4), 469–484.

Goldfarb, K. P., & Grinberg, J. (2002). Leadership for social justice: Authentic participation in the case of a community center in Caracas, Venezuela. *Journal of School Leadership, 12*(2), 157–173.

Hackman, M., & Johnson, C. (2000). *Leadership: A communication perspective.* Long Grove, IL: Waveland.

Hargreaves, A., Earl, L., Moore, S., & Manning, S. (2000). *Learning to change.* San Francisco: Jossey-Bass.

Heifetz, R. (1994). *Leadership without easy answers.* Cambridge, MA: Harvard University Press.

Heifetz, R., Grasgow, A., & Linksy, M. (2009). *The practice of adaptive leadership.* Cambridge, MA: Harvard Business School Press.

Hirsch, E. D. (1999). *The schools we need: And why we do not have them.* New York: Anchor.

hooks, b. (1994). *Teaching to transgress.* New York: Routledge.

Intrator, S., & Kunzman, R. (2006, Fall). The person in the profession: Renewing teacher vitality through professional development. *The Educational Forum, 71,* 16–32.

Korthagen, F. (2004). In search of the essence of a good teacher: Towards a more holistic approach in teacher education. *Teaching and Teacher Education, 2004*(20), 77–97.

Korthagen, F., & Vasalos, A. (2005). Levels in reflection: Core reflection as a means to enhance professional growth. *Teachers and Teaching: Theory and Practice, 11*(1), 47–71.

Korthagen, F., & Vasalos, A. (2008, March). *Quality from within as the key to professional development.* Paper presented at the Annual Meeting of the American Educational Research Association, New York.

Kouzes, J., & Posner, B. (2002). *The leadership challenge.* San Francisco: Jossey-Bass.

Kouzes, J., & Posner, B. (2003a). *Credibility.* San Francisco: Jossey-Bass.

Kouzes, J., & Posner, B. (2003b). *Encouraging the heart.* San Francisco: Jossey-Bass.

Levine, A. (2005). *Educating school leaders*. Washington, DC: Education Schools Project.

Lindsey, R., Nuri Robins, K., & Terrell, R. (2003). *Cultural proficiency*. Thousand Oaks, CA: Corwin.

Marshall, C., & Olivia, M. (2006). *Leadership for social justice*. Boston: Pearson.

Marshall, C., & Ward, M. (2004). "Yes, but . . .": Education leaders discuss social justice. *Journal of School Leadership, 14*(3), 530–563.

Maxwell, J. C. (1993). *Developing the leader within you*. Nashville: Nelson Business.

Michelli, N., & Keiser, D. L. (2005). *Teacher education for democracy and education*. New York: Routledge.

Palmer, P. J. (1998a). *The courage to teach*. San Francisco: Jossey-Bass.

Palmer, P. J. (1998b). Leading from within. In L. Spears (Ed.), *Insights on leadership* (pp. 197–208). New York: Wiley.

Palmer, P. J. (2004). *A hidden wholeness*. San Francisco: Jossey-Bass.

Postman, N. (1996). *The end of education*. New York: Vintage Press.

Scharmer, O. (2007). *Theory U: Leading from the future as it emerges*. Cambridge, MA: Society for Organizational Learning.

Senge, P. M. (1990). *The fifth discipline*. New York: Currency Doubleday.

Terrell, R., & Lindsey, R. (2008). *Culturally proficient leadership*. Thousand Oaks, CA: Corwin.

Theoharis, G. T. (2004). *At no small cost: Social justice leaders and their response to resistance*. Unpublished doctoral dissertation, University of Wisconsin–Madison.

Thompson, M. (2000). *The congruent life*. San Francisco: Jossey-Bass.

Yukl, G. (2006). *Leadership in organizations* (6th ed.). Upper Saddle River, NJ: Pearson-Prentice Hall.

Leadership for Transformation

The Work of the Worm

Mark Nepo

The story is told by a member of the Ojibway tribe that the Great Spirit had trouble keeping the world together, when a little worm said he could help. Knowing that the secret of life lived in everything, the Great Spirit welcomed the little worm's help. So the Great Spirit said, "Help me little worm" and the little worm slowly spun its barely seeable silk, connecting all of creation with a delicate web. The Great Spirit smiled and Its smile cast a light across the earth, making the web of connection briefly visible. The Great Spirit marveled at the little worm's industrious gift. For the worm was not clever or brilliant but simply devoted to being and doing what it was put here to do; to inch through the earth, spinning from its guts a fine thread that holds everything together. And so the Great Spirit said to the little worm, "You have saved us little worm, not by being great or bold, but by staying true to your own nature. I will let you live forever."

The little worm was stunned and somewhat frightened. The Great Spirit saw this, "Don't you want to live forever?" The little worm inched closer, "Oh Father, the earth is big enough to cross. I fear so many years if I can't grow." The Great Spirit smiled again at the wisdom of one of Its smallest creatures.

"Very well, little worm, I will only let you grow into forever. I will give you the ability to spin this precious thread that connects everything around yourself. When you can enclose yourself within that web and quiet your urge to inch and squirm away, you will emerge after a time with the thinnest of wings full of color. Then you will know the lightness of being that I know." The little worm bowed and began to search for a leaf on which to grow. And this is how the Great Spirit enabled the worm to spin a cocoon and from its quietude become a butterfly.

Building Bridges to Transform Lives

An Integrative Leadership Response to the "Wicked Problem" of Homelessness

John Blenkinsopp

This chapter is a case study of leadership that sought to tackle the "wicked problem" of homelessness. I draw upon the integrative public leadership literature, which examines how public problems can be addressed through leadership that engages with a complex network of actors across multiple organizations (Bryson & Crosby, 2008; Crosby & Bryson, 2005b; Huxham, 2003; Huxham & Vangen, 2000). Despite acknowledgment of the need for inter-organizational collaboration to address public issues, leaders are still typically tasked with agendas that assume an "in-charge" model of organization (Crosby & Bryson, 2005a). There is an urgent need to understand how leaders can practice integrative public leadership while working within the constraints of the role demands placed upon them. I therefore examine how leaders in a particular organization managed to exert an influence well beyond its boundaries, building bridges with other stake-holders to effectively transform the lives of a particular section of society. That organization was Tyneside Cyrenians (TCUK), a charity in the northeast of England dedicated to supporting homeless people; their mission statement is "Changing Lives, Building Futures." I selected this organization because it had been conspicuously successful in achieving its aims, with leaders clearly identified as drivers of this success, which was accomplished through leadership activities across sectors. The

Cyrenians, however, remained recognizably a single organization and not a cross-sector collaborative venture, previously the main focus of research in this field.

Integrative Public Leadership

Integrative public leadership is leadership that fosters collective action across many types of boundaries in order to achieve the common good, with the boundaries between sectors of society the main focus (Crosby & Bryson, 2005a). Bryson and Crosby suggest that the stimulus for cross-sector collaboration is failure: "Only when single-sector solutions fail or prove inadequate . . . do leaders, policymakers, and activists turn to cross-sector collaboration" (2008, p. 55). Drawing upon the notion of wicked problems, scholars note that attempts to solve such problems through single-sector solutions are likely to fail (Clarke & Stewart, 1997; Keast, Mandell, Brown, & Woolcock, 2004; Roberts, 2000). Homelessness is a particularly wicked problem and requires integrative public leadership that bridges the boundaries across all five major sectors of society (business, government, nonprofit, media, and community), illustrated by the organizations whose actions have an impact on homelessness, such as banks, chambers of commerce, courts, drug treatment clinics, grocery stores, hospitals, liquor stores, local government, the military, neighborhood watch schemes, newspapers, the police, prisons, private landlords, the probation (parole) service, and TV stations.

The Wicked Problem of Homelessness

Herb Rittel first proposed the distinction between tame and wicked problems, suggesting that problems tackled by engineers and scientists are "tame" as they have a clarity about the nature of the problem and thus about whether a solution had been achieved. By contrast, policy and planning problems have no solution. Among the ten properties of wicked problems (Rittel & Webber, 1973), four are particularly relevant to homelessness.

First, there is no definitive formulation of a wicked problem. Considerable debate exists about what constitutes homelessness. Mortgage problems are a common cause for people losing their homes, but only a small subset of this group would be viewed by government agencies as homeless. Similarly, families forced to leave their homes by natural disasters are typically viewed as temporarily without accommodation rather than homeless. Homelessness policy is usually focused on "rough sleepers"—people who are not merely without a home of their own but are actually sleeping rough (in shop doorways, "cardboard cities," and so on). Yet those working with homeless people know there are a range of forms of homelessness.

Second, every wicked problem can be considered to be a symptom of another problem. Even after narrowing the focus to rough sleepers, the problem remains complex because there are differing perspectives on the nature of the problem faced. Most rough sleepers live chaotic lives in which homelessness is a by-product of their inability to engage with social systems (work, family, education, and so on). Homelessness can be seen as a secondary issue, resolved by providing the rough sleeper with hostel accommodation, thus allowing the individual and relevant agencies to address the "real" problem(s), for example, drug addiction or mental illness. These underlying problems, however, frequently are *also* wicked problems and thus, for example, efforts to address the wicked problem of homelessness for people with drug problems is influenced by policy debates about the best way to tackle the wicked problem of drug abuse.

Third, there are numerous competing explanations for the wicked problem, with the choice of explanation determining the choice of solution. Multiple causes of homelessness include recent examples such as unemployment leading people to move in search of work, closure of long-stay mental hospitals in favor of community care, a lack of affordable rental accommodation, and service personnel discharged in the aftermath of war. There is a risk that different stakeholders focus on a particular cause as the dominant explanation, with subsequent policy debates being driven by this interpretation. Bryson and Crosby (2008) note that efforts to create cross-sector collaboration arise from failure, and we can certainly view homelessness as a failure of our social systems; however, this failure may not trigger collaboration if there is dispute about the very nature of the failure (and what should be done about it).

Finally, every wicked problem is essentially unique. Those who work with the homeless acquire a deep knowledge of this complex issue, knowledge that is often local and specific. Tackling homelessness on Tyneside will be very different from tackling the issue in London or Cairo or New York. While things can be learned from practice elsewhere, there is no "solution" that can be copied.

When one understands the reasons why homelessness is a wicked problem, one can see the need for leadership in developing a consensus on the nature of the problem, generating possible solutions, and gaining cross-sector buy-in for efforts to implement these solutions. Additionally, given the added complexity that homelessness has unique causes and solutions in each locality, a clarity and boldness of vision is required from leaders seeking to address this problem in a given location, since they are not seeking to persuade others to adopt solutions tested elsewhere but to take a leap of faith in taking the steps they believe are best suited to transforming the local situation.

Methodology

Having previously undertaken research with Tyneside Cyrenians on a different issue, I had insights into the organization's relevance as a case study for exploring integrative leadership. I gathered data from several sources. Internal documents, combined with a detailed organizational profile compiled by an external body provided a great deal of the contextual information, which is crucial to any attempt to understand leadership (Bryman, Stephens, & Campo, 1996). Interviews with key internal and external stakeholders helped me to understand how, from their different perspectives, the "story" unfolded over time. All of the participants had been involved in the homeless scene on Tyneside during this period. My prior research provided information on the experiences of relatively junior staff and how these staff located their work within the emerging ideas on how the organization might contribute to addressing homelessness.

Organizational History and Context

Tyneside Cyrenians was formed in 1970 by a group of people concerned about the lack of facilities for people who were "sleeping rough." Starting with a soup run each evening, TCUK developed its first hostel in 1972, and during the next two decades built up its relationships with local housing associations and the city council. By the end of the 1990s, the organization looked like many other large service providers across the United Kingdom: sheltering vulnerable people, helping them access basic services, but paying limited attention to helping them move on to independent living. This approach, known colloquially as "heads on beds," was challenged toward the end of the 1990s when the new Labour government signaled a shift of focus in dealing with homelessness. This policy shift acted as a trigger for change, and TCUK management began to look beyond just providing accommodation and started thinking about taking a more strategic approach. In 1998 they opened a Day Centre to help people access services and productive activities, and in 2000 piloted a project to match up homeless people with hostel spaces across the different providers within Newcastle. Such arrangements are crucial for making efficient use of resources, and the project became such an integral part of the Tyneside homelessness scene it was later taken over by the local council. In the case study I examine the period from the end of the 1990s onward, focusing on changes that resulted from the introduction of the government's new policy on homelessness ("Supporting People") in 2002.

The central issue in Supporting People was not homelessness but housing benefits and the way they were paid. Organizations like TCUK had always received housing benefit payments for their residents, and these payments were supposed to cover both rent and the cost of providing support to residents. However, as there were no serious checks on the level of support provided, organizations varied widely in how much support they offered their service users. The Supporting People policy separated the payments for rent and support and set out clear rules about what organizations had to do in order to continue to qualify for the support payment. The essence of the new policy was therefore a shift away from funding long-term residence in accommodation for homeless people and toward supporting them to live independently. It seems a logical idea: if someone is homeless, offer them temporary accommodation and support until they can get back on their feet and into their own accommodation. Critics of the policy, however, argue that it greatly underestimates the extent to which homeless people typically have a range of problems; homelessness itself is often just one of several overlapping needs/problems. In a recent survey of service users, almost half had issues with alcohol, a third had drug issues, a third were ex-offenders, a fifth had mental health problems, and a small number had learning disabilities. Some service users will have a combination of such issues; one might be an ex-offender with a drug addiction and mental health problems, for example. Yet Supporting People was built on an assumption that organizations such as TCUK can take people from rough sleeping to being able to rent their own place in an average of three months. This incredibly challenging target provided a major driver for change.

Prior to Supporting People, each of the seven providers on Tyneside dealing with homeless people tended to focus on specific groups; for example, ex-offenders, drug addicts, and alcoholics. There was a history of reasonably close working relationships; it was common practice for new staff to be provided with a list of contacts at the other organizations and told to get to know them. This cooperative approach started to break down in the late 1990s, when the sector first became aware of the policy ideas that would eventually crystallize into Supporting People. This period was a difficult one—providers could see that funding was going to change radically and perceived they would be in competition with each other to obtain it. The only funding stream that seemed likely to be reliable was that specifically earmarked for homelessness, which meant providers felt they had to "rebadge" themselves as service providers for homeless people—"It was less risky because nobody knew what the priorities were going to be" (operations manager). In some cases, reorienting to this new funding stream meant a shift away from the provider's traditional key stakeholders; the probation (parole) service, traditionally a key stakeholder, became much less prominent within the sector. The shift to a superficially more homogenous sector only added to the anxiety about competition; now that providers were more similar, would it be easier for funding bodies to channel monies to the "best" providers, leading to mergers or takeovers? The policy Supporting People was followed by the introduction of the Quality Assessment Framework (QAF) process, which examined provider performance in supporting homeless people toward independent living. Providers saw how much work was required to assess seven separate organizations and concluded that the QAF process was likely to lead to fewer providers as the weakest providers were closed or taken over. Each therefore strove to ensure its own organization got the best ratings to guarantee continued funding, increasing perceptions of being in competition with the other providers. The extent to which the sector *dis*integrated during this period is an important backdrop to later efforts to work in a more integrative fashion.

Case Study Findings

The complexity of the case study led me to draw out themes as they emerged progressively from the data, following the approach adopted by Mouly and Sankaran (1999). I identified three themes that appeared particularly significant—leading a visibly effective organization, networking and influencing, and engaging in shaping policy—but their separation for purposes of analysis and exposition should not be assumed to indicate a separation in reality. The activities captured under each theme can be seen to be linked from the outset, eventually coming to form an integrated whole in terms of the strategy and operations of the organization.

Leading a Visibly Effective Organization

To take an integrative public leadership role, the TCUK senior team would need to be seen to be running a highly effective organization. (By 2001 it badly needed to rebuild its reputation locally.) To be credible in shaping or influencing the agenda, especially if offering its own work as an example, it needed to be perceived as innovative and as delivering a good service. Yet in the short run, the CEO recalls, the organization had no such high-flown considerations—they simply needed money! Government had increasingly adopted a funding model in which providers had to bid for funds from specific initiatives, and this required the organization to develop skills and expertise in writing bids and managing bid-funded projects. Only gradually did their efforts, focused largely on an anxious search for alternative sources of funding, coalesce into a clear strategic focus.

The changing environment for homeless charities coincided with a period of uncertainty in the management structure at

TCUK. In 2001, a new CEO was appointed. He was an internal appointment, having been the finance manager since 1984. Though he was already keen to implement change in the organization, the need to respond to the requirements of Supporting People forced him to implement a whole raft of major changes almost immediately. Many staff, largely unaware of the implications of the new policy, perceived the various changes he sought to introduce as being part of his personal agenda rather than a necessary response to changes in government policy. If Supporting People represented a significant shift in the funding arrangements, the shift in organizational culture demanded by the policy was even more profound. Prior to this time, many service users were long-stay residents, who had been in TCUK so long that it was unrealistic to expect them ever to move out. The newly arrived service users tended to be much younger; many had drug problems and were generally more challenging in their behavior than the older residents. Staff used to dealing with the older kind of service user did not always have the skills to provide the combination of challenge and support needed to help service users progress quickly to independent living.

The changes to the structure of the organization, and the nature of its work, led to considerable resistance from staff. Many existing work practices were inefficient and ineffective, but some of these were attractive to the staff. It had become common practice, for example, for staff to be provided with meals even though the catering budget was supposed to be for the service users, to a point where some staff would order high-quality food for themselves and cheap food for service users. On the negative side, staff had previously been expected to perform a number of activities for no payment, for example, come in on their days off to do any training, or accompany service users on weekends away. The aim was to move to a more professional way of working—so, no extra work without payment or time off, but no free meals either. Perhaps, inevitably, many staff focused on what they had lost rather than what they had gained, and the first year or so involved "a lot of head-on battles" between the CEO and staff: "I've had petitions given to me and all sorts. I remember a famous one was signed by 'The Staff,' but I knew from the inside that it had come from just five members of staff so I wrote back to all of the staff, copying in the letter I'd received from 'The Staff' and there was an uproar; it was one of the best things I ever did" (CEO).

Though difficult at the time, these "battles" proved necessary to communicate clearly to staff that things had really changed. Some embraced the changes from the start, and others eventually came around to what the organization was doing. Some left and were replaced by new staff who did not know anything about the old ways of working and accepted the new culture from day one. Despite clear leadership and a range of HR activities aimed at changing culture, it still took many years to reach a point where the vast majority of staff could be described as supportive of the new culture and ways of working.

Networking and Influencing

The subsequent expansion of TCUK required a development in the management structure, with new professional roles in areas such as fund raising, public relations, HR, and so on. The CEO was very proactive in recruiting to these roles, in some cases head-hunting or poaching key staff from other organizations, a practice common in business but highly unusual in the voluntary sector and somewhat controversial. This head-hunting or poaching represented a response to the strategic driver to diversify funding: by recruiting staff with a variety of expert knowledge and access to key networks, TCUK could operate with a much more complete understanding of the strategic environment. This improved knowledge base and better networks meant they were aware of, and in a better position to access, a much broader range of funding sources. They also provided a source of new ideas and perspectives, encouraging TCUK to develop initiatives very different from its original core business, and raised the profile of the organization by plugging it into a greater range of networks.

Using its networks, TCUK has been active in bringing together different sectors—public, private, and voluntary—to work on the problem of homelessness through a range of networking activities, both speculative and purposive. A good example of this coalition building through networking was the CEO's attempts to get involved in a national network on homelessness by attending the annual general meeting (AGM). He was astonished when the poorly attended AGM was over in fifteen minutes; but as the stranger in their midst, he stood out and was approached by board members curious as to why he had come. This brief encounter led to an invitation to be the northeast of England representative, instantly locating him within a well-connected network, and he eventually became a full board member. More speculative networking included involvement in the local Chamber of Commerce, in the Academy of Chief Executives network, and taking a guest spot reviewing the newspapers on local radio.

I now turn to a consideration of the outcomes of the networking and illustrate the central role of networking behavior in achieving the integrative public leadership observed in the case study.

Shaping the Policy Agenda

The difficulties experienced in responding to Supporting People underlined how reactive the leadership was, not only in TCUK but within each of the homelessness organizations throughout Tyneside. In a sense, most of the key developments it triggered (networking, culture change, management restructuring) have been an attempt by TCUK to wrestle the agenda back toward the organization. The emphasis has been placed on *action* rather than *reaction*. The engagement with key government agencies on the implementation of Supporting People offers a useful illustration of this theme. Though initially wanting merely to gain a better understanding of the policy, the CEO quickly realized the provider organizations had a better understanding of the policy implications than did government. By getting involved early, TCUK risked being roundly criticized by the inspection process, but it took that risk on the basis that it would be the first provider to understand the process and could therefore have an influence on it (and also steal a march on other providers). This engagement with government on Supporting People can be seen as the start of the emphasis on external networking described in the previous section of the chapter.

The senior team at TCUK are modest about the extent to which they have shaped the homelessness agenda, yet in key areas they made significant progress in reordering policy priorities. "I think there are things we have shaped thinking and we've consciously set out to do that, to make sure that the services we provide, and are looking to provide, are high on the agenda. . . . We certainly weren't preaching about it, we were saying this is what we're doing and it's a good way of working" (Operations Manager). The senior team perceive themselves as shaping the opinions of policymakers as much as policies; an example of this approach involved the CEO leading a party of local politicians around the city center at 2:00 a.m. on a winter's night to talk to the homeless people they found. As he dryly notes, "That sort of stuff does change the way people think about things." Tyneside Cyrenians have also become adept at making a noise in favor of neglected client groups. For example, most rough sleepers are men, but there is a significant minority of women whose needs were never considered as part of the strategy against homelessness in the region. The senior team appear to be skilled at judging when issues relevant to their service users are starting to come to the attention of policymakers and know that coming along with "answers" at a time when policymakers are just starting to work out what the questions should be allows them to exert an influence on policy development. However, they are also pragmatic and know when to back down over politically sensitive issues. Sometimes the policy climate is simply not receptive to an issue, and as a small organization they lack the time and resources to keep pressing, though like all good leaders they take the long view: describing a failure to change a key element of drugs policy, the Operations Manager notes, "In three or four years I'll start pushing again."

Further Developments

We noted the CEO's caution about viewing developments at TCUK during his first few years in office as anything more than a harried response to the need to secure funding, but a more deliberately strategic and integrative leadership gradually emerged through management (and service users) pushing forward a range of nonresidential services in two areas: social inclusion, and training and employment. Through its social inclusion strand, TCUK developed opportunities for volunteering at its day center, reaching out to sex workers, and won a prestigious contract from the Social Exclusion Task Force to pilot a street outreach service staffed entirely by formerly homeless people. Reaching out to and supporting homeless people can pose significant challenges, particularly with those who become entrenched and institutionalized. They can be distrustful of authority and worried that getting help from the state or even a charity will get them entangled with the police; this is a particular worry for sex workers. Mental health problems compound the difficulty. Tyneside Cyrenians placed particular emphasis on trying to engage with hard-to-reach groups, breaking down suspicion and building up trust.

Training and employability has been a second focus. One of the hidden challenges of Supporting People was finding agencies willing to help service users access training and employment, which are key to living independently in the long term. Homeless people typically have poor educational qualifications; often they dropped out of school and are suspicious of classrooms and teachers. Some have not been in employment for years and lack basic skills, such as time keeping or communication, needed to hold down a job. Traditionally, the focus was on getting people into jobs or education without necessarily equipping them with the skills to stay in those jobs; but homeless people typically need time to build up skills and self-confidence through training schemes and work placements as well as support for job retention. Tyneside Cyrenians therefore embarked on a "self-build" project in partnership with a construction firm, employing twelve homeless people to build new offices at TCUK headquarters as a means to support them in getting qualifications and valuable experience in construction. This scheme provided the foundation for the development of a more extensive training and employment service by TCUK. It has also been active in employing ex-service users, going from two ex-service users in a staff of forty in 2003 to thirty-five in a staff of about one hundred in 2009. The ways in which these initiatives have been implemented show that the TCUK senior team are very streetwise—although their actions were principled, the managers also ensured they maximized their potential as a public relations coup, seeking business opportunities, tapping into additional funding, and so on.

One important aspect of all of these changes is their novelty. These developments were not merely new to TCUK but new within the sector, and this provided a significant leadership challenge: to develop new services without any existing examples of good practice upon which they could be modeled. At the same time, the very novelty of their innovations has contributed to the organization's efforts to position itself as an excellent and innovative service provider.

Conclusion

Homelessness is part of such an entrenched series of social ills that any attempt to tackle the issue involves an almost heroic sense of mission. It is an integrative problem, often the result of a number of different elements at the level of the individual (for example, drug and alcohol addiction, domestic violence, parental abuse) and society (for example, government policy, housing and labor markets). Tyneside Cyrenians has managed to integrate public, private, and voluntary sectors on a number of levels—national, regional, and local—and positioned itself as one of the leading players in the region's homelessness network. One of the key stakeholders from a local government agency praised TCUK for its competence, clear vision, and track record of delivery when she stated, "They always have the whole plan before they commit to it . . . and that gives you a bit of certainty." The organization also has a reputation for innovations that anticipate the changing needs of the homeless, often running ahead of current policy, and frequently finance these innovations through new sources of funding. Tyneside Cyrenians continues to try and forge strategic links with other voluntary organizations and works with central government bodies as well as agencies such as the police and drug treatment centers. They have embraced private businesses, working in partnership with building firms in the self-build scheme, and pitching their work to corporate philanthropists in novel ways.

The focus of this chapter was on understanding how leaders engage in integrative public leadership from within the bounds of their own organizations. This case study suggests that TCUK achieved a great deal, with its leaders as key to the accomplishments, often through numerous acts of influence. Many of the changes that TCUK needed from other key stakeholders (such as funding bodies and local government) were so minor that their actions in obtaining the necessary changes from these stakeholders were almost certainly not recognized by the stakeholders (or TCUK) as acts of integrative leadership. Yet their actions produced an appreciable impact on addressing the wicked problem of homelessness. Taken together, these actions gave TCUK a position of strength, as a key node in the network from which to press on with the greater challenge of shaping the agenda on homelessness. There was little evidence of full-scale collaboration; instead the TCUK senior team were engaged in extensive networking and relationship building, a vital activity within a sector that has experienced disintegration. In building links with organizations, they also create links *between* organizations—even if at the outset that link is merely both having dealings with TCUK. An important area for future research would be to examine this process, to understand how these links can be forged and strengthened through the actions of an organization that acts as an inadvertent matchmaker (perhaps becoming more deliberate over time).

The organization succeeded in shifting attitudes and behavior in many important ways, increasing their service users' access to employment opportunities, housing, and a range of social services. The considerable success of the organization in achieving its aims underscores the value of studying the process by which these leaders enacted integrative public leadership. Led by an exceptionally strong and clear-sighted CEO, who took over an organization about which few people cared, the CEO and his senior team leveraged the lack of interest into great freedom to do what they thought was right, largely unfettered by stakeholder constraints. Such situations are increasingly rare: it is difficult to imagine the CEO of a hospital or a listed company being given such latitude. So, while this case study has provided some insights into how a single organization and its leaders can affect integrative public leadership, we need further studies to understand how this might be done under less supportive conditions.

Acknowledgments

I am very grateful to senior staff at Tyneside Cyrenians for providing access. Readers interested in finding out more about this inspiring organization are encouraged to browse their highly informative Web site: www.thecyrenians.org.

References

Bryman, A., Stephens, M., & Campo, C. A. (1996). The importance of context: Qualitative research and the study of leadership. *The Leadership Quarterly, 7*, 353–370.

Bryson, J. M., & Crosby, B. C. (2008). Failing into cross-sector collaboration successfully. In L. B. Bingham & R. O'Leary (Eds.), *Big ideas in collaborative public management* (pp. 55–78). Armonk, NY: M. E. Sharpe.

Clarke, M., & Stewart, J. (1997). *Handling the wicked issues: A challenge for government.* Birmingham, UK: University of Birmingham, Institute for Local Government Studies.

Crosby, B. C., & Bryson, J. M. (2005a). *Leadership for the common good: Tackling public problems in a shared-power world* (2nd ed.). San Francisco: Jossey-Bass.

Crosby, B. C., & Bryson, J. M. (2005b). A leadership framework for cross-sector collaboration. *Public Management Review, 7*(2), 177–201.

Huxham, C. (2003). Theorizing collaboration practice. *Public Management Review, 5*(3), 401–423.

Huxham, C., & Vangen, S. (2000). Leadership in the shaping and implementation of collaboration agendas: How things happen in a (not quite) joined-up world. *The Academy of Management Journal, 43*(6), 1159–1175.

Keast, R., Mandell, M., Brown, K., & Woolcock, G. (2004). Network structures: Working differently and changing expectations. *Public Administration Review, 64*(3), 363–371.

Mouly, V. S., & Sankaran, J. K. (1999). The "permanent" acting leader: Insights from a dying Indian R&D organization. *The Leadership Quarterly, 10*, 637–665.

Rittel, H. W. J., & Webber, M. M. (1973). Dilemmas in a general theory of planning. *Policy Sciences, 4*, 155–169.

Roberts, N. C. (2000). Coping with wicked problems: The case of Afghanistan. *Learning from International Public Management Reform, 11B*, 353–375.

Virtual Communication, Transformational Leadership, Personality, and the Apparent Holographic Constructs of Implicit Leadership

Charles Salter, Mark Green, Phyllis A. Duncan, Anne Berre, and Charles Torti

Early leadership researchers acknowledged that effective leadership is dependent upon the characteristics of the *leader* and the *situation* (Southwell, Anghelcev, Himelboim, & Jones, 2007). Unquestionably, communication technologies have drastically changed the work environment (situation) and presented new challenges for effective leadership. For example, at least 10 percent of the workforce is currently working in virtual settings or telecommuting from home (CNN Reports, 2007), and 42 percent of all companies nationwide offer telecommuting as an alternative form of full-time employment ("Survey," 2008). The virtual work environment is one of the many situations forever changed by the technology evolution. It is essential that virtualization be considered a key social process rather than mere technological advancements as suggested by Diemers (1998). Virtual team leaders and members should learn to utilize facilitation techniques that work for virtual teams. Technology, for example, cannot make up for unprepared or ill-conceived meetings (Duarte & Snyder, 2001); managers still need to manage and leaders still need to lead even in a virtual environment. The question we should be concerned with is, What methods or leadership styles can leaders utilize to motivate followers with whom we will never have face-to-face communication in a virtual setting?

While there has been little research on how virtual communications affect the individual leader-follower relationship, studies on transformational leadership in groups and virtual environments have led to findings that indicate that higher levels of transformational leadership lead to group effectiveness (Hoyt & Blascovich, 2003; Sosik, Avolio, Kahai, & Jung, 1998). Additionally, Cassell, Huffaker, Tversky, and Ferriman (2006) found that teenagers emerge as leaders in virtual online e-mail communications by using language that referred to group goals rather than themselves.

Perceptibly, transformational leadership and the manner in which we work together are also changing. Most agree that transformational leaders are charismatic and arouse others' enthusiasm, loyalty, and trust in themselves (Schermerhorn, 2002). Traditionally, charismatic leaders have built trust through face-to-face environments. Distance workers tend to believe that no news is bad news, and consequently the lack of interactions erodes trust (Fisher & Fisher, 2001). These same authors also restate the recommendations of Robert Their, a manager at Xerox, who imbeds the pictures of team members into computer technology in order to replicate face-to-face environments. Others recommend trust be achieved through an open culture that shares information, cultivates teamwork, and promotes positive commitment to an organization's goal (Dess & Picken, 1999).

The virtual work environment triggers enthusiasm at first because employees are excited about the new arrangement; however, the fervor fades rapidly as one experiences the feeling of isolation. To counter these feelings, leaders should keep the knowledge transfer alive (Crandall & Wallace, 1998). Educators generally agree that students, similar to employees, often experience isolation if there is not a continual and open communication link. In presenting education modules via the Internet, Cree and Macaulay (2000) believe that the ability to convey encouragement and enthusiasm via the written word with no supportive nonverbal signals was a must. Regardless of whether the virtual environment is a business or educational institute, specific words or phrases to promote enthusiasm are necessary but often absent.

Since transformational leaders are enthusiastic and there is minimum research regarding these types of leadership skills and virtual communications (Agres, Edberg, & Igbaria, 1998), the focus of this study was to identify specific words or phrases associated with transformational leaders in virtual environments. The study further investigates the relationship between leaders' communications and followers' personality ratings, and followers' rating of the leaders based on the Full Range Leadership Model, as operationally measured by the MLQ (Multi-factor Leadership Questionnaire) (Bass & Avolio, 1994).

Transformational Leadership and Its Outcomes

Burns (1978) first identified transforming leaders as those leaders who motivated followers to high performance and change by using high moral values. Bass and Avolio (1994) identified the components of transformational leadership as

1. *Idealized influence*: Leaders serve as role models for their followers.
2. *Inspirational motivation*: Leaders motivate their followers and inspire those around them by giving meaning to followers' work.
3. *Intellectual stimulation*: Leaders stimulate followers by encouraging them to be creative and question old beliefs, and
4. *Individualized consideration*: Leaders attend to each follower's needs through two-way communication, as identified in their Full Range Leadership Model.

Over the years, researchers have found a correlation between transformational leadership and higher employee loyalty, trust, commitment, performance, and satisfaction (Dumdum, Lowe, & Avolio, 2002; Elenkov, 2002; Hoyt & Blascovich, 2003; Jung & Sosik, 2002; Kark & Shamir, 2002; Kark, Shamir, & Chen, 2003; LeBrasseur, Whissell, & Ojha, 2002; Rai & Sinha, 2000).

Personality Traits and Transformational Leadership

The personality of effective leaders has been well researched. From the studies of Raymond Cattell (1944), who studied personality characteristics in an attempt to connect leadership effectiveness and leader personality, to Tupes and Christal (1992), who combined Cattell's sixteen taxonomies into what we know as the "Big Five" personality traits of today, leaders' personality has been of primary importance as a guide for leadership researchers. Costa and McCrae (1988) continued research on these personality traits: extraversion, conscientiousness, openness to experience, neuroticism, and agreeableness; they concluded that a significant supply of these Big Five personality traits were those needed by successful individuals in business organizations. Salgado (1997) found that the Big Five Personality Model of traits was present in other cultures around the world and suggested a universality of these traits.

Avolio and Gibbons (1988) stated that while transformational leadership is a behavioral theory, it does not mean that these behaviors could not have their origin from an individual's background characteristics or traits. Bass (1990) suggested that if transformational leadership could be based on one's background characteristics or traits, then these traits were universal to humankind.

Ehrhart and Klein (2001) found that perceptions and attribution of transformational leadership are influenced by a follower's values and needs. Howell and Frost (1989) stated that personality traits could influence perception and acceptance of the leader.

Ehrhart and Klein (2001) further assert that the follower's personality traits, based on a perceived similarity between the follower and the leader, influenced the follower's preference for transformational leadership. Felfe and Schyns (2006) examined follower personality and how it related to follower perception of the leader and found that those followers who rated themselves high in extraversion tended to perceive the leader as more transformational than did followers with low extraversion.

Implicit and Transformational Leadership

The discussion on followers' expectancies of leader behavior or implicit leadership was begun by Eden and Leviathan (1975), who found that leader behaviors guide a perceiver's encoding of relevant information. Carlisle and Phillips (1984) found that the perceiver's formation of leadership perceptions was enhanced when a leader's traits were positively prototyped by the follower. Mischel (1977) suggested that traits are important as constructs for perceivers, which help them to organize perceptions of others. Winter and Uleman (1984) indicated that individuals unconsciously make trait inferences when encoding information into memory. Lord, De Vader, and Alliger (1986) concluded that research on implicit leadership theory indicates the relationship between the perceiver's cognitive schema fabricated by a leader's traits and their importance as perceptual constructs for perceivers. Lord and Maher (1991) found that a follower's recall of leadership information instructions is enhanced if the follower has correctly cognitively mapped or prototyped the leader's traits.

Keller (1992) stated that implicit leadership asks about the relationship between the evaluations and perceptions of leaders. Kark and Shamir (2002) asserted that transformational leaders have dual influence on followers, that transformational leaders' influence over the follower is derived by their ability to change the identities of followers through communication.

Identities, formed by personality traits, quality of relationships, and group norms that the leader influences, include the personal identity of the follower who models the leader and the social identity wherein the follower forms identification with the work unit. Additionally, Lord, Brown, and Freiberg (1999) suggested that implicit leadership theories were a category system that emphasized how prototypical behavior influenced the leadership perceptions and distortions in memory about leaders by perceivers.

Methodology

The central focus of this investigation was the relationship between the usage of words found in prior research to be those utilized by leaders rated above the mean as transformational leaders and words found to be used by leaders rated below the mean as transformational leaders (Salter, Carmody-Bubb, Duncan, & Green, 2007). The purpose of the study was to extract the influence of face-to-face communication in order to rate transformational leadership in a virtual setting.

Research Question

This study examined the degree to which followers' personality, as measured by the five-factor model of personality of Costa and McCrae (1988), is related to followers' ratings of the leader as a transformational leader, as assessed by the Multi-factor Leadership Questionnaire (MLQ-5X) published by Bass and Avolio (1994), in a virtual environmental setting. If followers' personalities predispose them to recognize one style of leadership when the leader is attempting to engage another style, theoretically this could result in miscommunications, faulty memory of instructions, and lack of employee security, all of which may lead to underperformance of the follower.

Participants

Since the focus of the study was the usage of certain words that were given in a communication, delivery of the survey was administered through the computer, in a classroom setting, and through e-mail. The sample for this study consisted of 306 respondents, university students, who were given two surveys, rendering a sample size of 612 responses. Participants consisted of 156 females and 150 males, with 92 percent 29 years of age or less, 3.9 percent between the ages of 30 and 43, with 4.1 percent between the ages of 44 and 51, from two universities. The ethnicity of the participants consisted of 219 white, 72 Spanish/Hispanic/Latino, 12 black/African American, and 3 Japanese.

Instruments and Operational Definitions

Three instruments were used in this study to define the independent and the dependent variables. Bass and Avolio's (1994) Full Range Leadership Model was operationally defined by the Multifactor Leadership Questionnaire. The MLQ-5X has been tested (Avolio, Bass, & Jung, 1999; Judge, Piccolo, & Ilies, 2004; Rowold & Herrera, 2003) and has been found to have reliability ratings of $r = .74$ to $r = .94$ and validity ratings between $r = .56$ and $r = .91$.

We used the International Personality Item Pool (IPIP) to rate the independent variable of the respondent's personality in virtual settings, when controlling for ethnicity, gender, and age. The IPIP is the equivalent of the Neuroticism Extraversion Openness to Experience Personality Inventory (NEO-PI) in measuring the Big Five, whose reliability and validity of these measures have been thoroughly investigated (Block, 1995; Costa & McCrae, 1988; Gough, 1990; Goldberg, 1990; John, 1990); and reliability scores range from $r = .86$ to $r = .95$ and validity correlates range from .77 to .92.

The dependent variable, leadership behavior, was assimilated with two scenarios using transformational and nontransformational language found by Salter and colleagues in a 2007 study. One scenario contained transformational words identified as Leader 1, and one scenario used transactional words identified as Leader 2.

Procedure

The questionnaire was administered to voluntary participants from two universities in Texas. The researchers delivered the anonymous data collection instrument in person, in a classroom setting, and through e-mail. Each respondent signed a detached informed consent notice prior to participation in the study. The collection instrument consisted of three parts. The first part was constructed of demographics, the success rating, and the two leader scenarios. The second part included two MLQ-5Xs: one to rate the leadership style of Leader 1, the virtual communication consisting of words considered utilized more on average by transformational leaders; and one to rate the leadership style of Leader 2, words utilized on average less by transformational leaders. The third instrument part consisted of the IPIP personality-rating instrument to rate the respondents themselves.

The virtual communication for Leader 1 consisted of approximately eighty words; eleven words were used from Transformational Leaders and Word Usage (see Table 12.1).

The words communicated by Leader 1 were those previously identified by Salter and colleagues (2007) as words associated with leaders scoring above the group mean as transformational leaders. The virtual scenario for Leader 2 consisted of seventy words, eight of which were taken from words previously utilized on average more often by leaders rated below the group mean for transformational leadership.

Table 12.1 Transformational Leaders and Word Usage

	Chi^2	P (2-tails)
Words Used More Frequently by Leaders below the Group Mean for Transformational Leadership		
Don't	46.46	0.00
Schedule	26.67	0.00
Tell	21.70	0.00
Time	13.38	0.00
Focused	13.33	0.00
Performance	9.34	0.01
More	8.51	0.01
Employee	7.35	0.03
Words Used More Frequently by Leaders above the Group Mean for Transformational Leadership		
Encourage	19.39	0.00
Fun	13.50	0.00
Future	10.80	0.01
Effort	10.00	0.01
Expected	10.00	0.01
Order	10.00	0.01
Plan	10.00	0.01
Listen	9.01	0.01
Teammates	8.10	0.02
Results	6.41	0.04
Brainstorm	5.40	0.05

Results

Respondents rated the Leader 1 virtual communication, which utilized previously identified transformational language (Salter et al., 2007), as significantly more transformational than the Leader 2 communication that used words not associated with transformational leaders. Participants who scored high in the Big Five personality traits of agreeableness, openness to experience, conscientiousness, and extraversion rated the leader as more transformational, while those high in neuroticism rated the leader as less transformational.

Transformational Ratings

Initially a univariate analysis of variance of the two virtual communications, as presented in Table 12.2, indicated that there was a significant difference in the transformational leadership ratings of Leader 1 and Leader 2. A significant interaction also existed for transformational speech and gender, $p < .05$, $F(1, 610) = 24.91$.

Further analysis of the mean scores indicated respondents found the virtual communication from Leader 1 to be significantly more transformational, with a mean transformational rating of 3.289 and a mean difference of 1.048, than the virtual communication from Leader 2, with a mean rating of 2.241, as shown in Table 12.3 and Figure 12.1.

Table 12.2 Analysis of Variance for Transformational Ratings

Variable	df	F	Sig.
TFSpeech	1	65.187	.000
Gender	1	.493	.483
Ethnicity	3	.472	.702
TFSpeech * Gender	1	24.916	.000
TFSpeech * Ethnicity	3	2.184	.089
Gender * Ethnicity	1	1.951	.163

Table 12.3 Scheffe Post Hoc Test for Transformational Ratings

Leaders	Mean Difference	Std. Error	Sig.
Leader 1	1.048	.103	.000
Leader 2	−1.048	.103	.000

Figure 12.1 Estimated Marginal Means of Transformational Rating by Transformational Speech

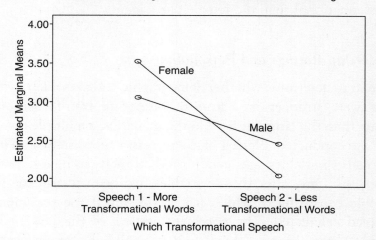

Estimated Marginal Means of Transformational Rating

Figure 12.2 Estimated Marginal Means of Transformational Rating by Gender

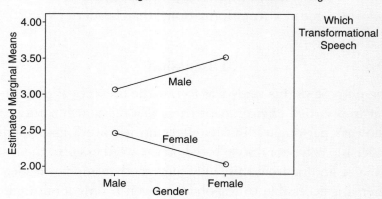

Estimated Marginal Means of Transformational Rating

As presented in Figure 12.2, a further investigation of the mean differences based on gender shows that males found Leader 1 (the communication utilizing words associated with leaders who score above the mean for transformational leadership) to be less transformational than did females. Noted on the same figure is the result that males found Leader 2 (the communication utilizing words associated with leaders who score below the mean for transformational leadership) to be more transformational than did female participants.

Leadership Ratings and Personality

In order to determine whether demographic and personality variables were stronger predictors of ratings of transformational ratings than the language used in the scenarios, a multiple regression was conducted. Block 1 of the regression consisted of all five personality variables, age, gender, and ethnicity using a stepwise regression. Only after those variables had been tested was the variable consisting of which leader (scenario) the participant received calculated. The conscientiousness of the participant ($R^2 = .01$, $r_p = .13$, $p = .01$) was a very small but positive predictor of ratings of transformational leadership. The language used by the leader in the scenario, however, was an extremely large predictor ($\Delta R^2 = .42$, $t = -21.60$, $p = .00$). Leader 1 (M = 3.289) was considered more transformational than Leader 2 (M = 2.241).

Discussion

The purpose of this study was to test the theoretical proposition that in a virtual environment there is a relationship between a follower's personality and its effect on follower's assessment of leadership behavioral style based on the word usage of the leader. A major finding from this study suggests that implicit leadership schema is accessible to respondents even if only a minimum of communication occurs in the absence of face-to-face communication. These findings suggest that women react to word usage more radically than men when assigning transformational ratings to virtual leaders or leaders with whom they have no face-to-face interaction. When using all of the independent variables in a multiple regression, the message was clear: Language is highly predictive of ratings of how transformational a leader is perceived to be, even when using virtual communication.

These findings were somewhat surprising as one thinks of transformational leadership as a very hands-on, face-to-face style of leadership. While the findings appear to be incongruent with our intuition and knowledge of transformational leaders, perhaps they can best be explained through the utilization of implicit leadership theories, followers' leadership schema, and Pribram's (1969) explanation of memory.

Lord, Brown, and Freiberg (1999) and Pribram (1977) suggest that even small portions of behavior, perhaps even single-word communications, in the absence of further communication, might elicit from the follower a prototypical implicit-based leadership style stored in his or her holographic memory. As suggested by Eden and Leviathan (1975), if leader behaviors guide memory of small tasks, then it might be plausible to suggest that a small prototypical behavior could guide a follower's assessment of a leader's leadership style.

The importance of this research to organizational leaders is relevant to a better understanding of motivational language, followers' personality traits, and these traits' propensity or lack of propensity to influence followers' perceptions of a leader's style. Leaders change styles in order to better motivate their followers to higher productivity. If leaders utilize language that is readily associated by followers as a leadership style, then leaders may learn to utilize communication to motivate and engage followers in a virtual setting. Also, if followers' personality and perception of leadership effectiveness and styles can be established, then leaders could more productively communicate leadership styles to followers of varying personality.

Recommendations for Future Research

These findings should be limited to the convenience sample from which they were taken. Convenience sampling consisting of only those seeking a higher education in a population might not be representative of the population as a whole. Therefore, these findings are not necessarily similar to the findings of a representative sample of the entire population. This study should be repeated with a more representative sample.

In the future, scholars should look further into implicit leadership theory and its effect on the behavior of the follower, the personality traits of followers, and the relationship those behaviors have with follower motivation. Full investigation of leadership behaviors and followers' perception is an interdisciplinary pursuit that blends the disciplines of psychology, physiology, neurology, verbal and nonverbal communication, and leadership studies into more encompassing theories of leadership.

Research raises a number of questions as researchers try to answer two or three questions. As often happens with research, some questions are asked and answered, while additional questions are raised. In conclusion, we finish this study with a question for a new line of research: What is it about leadership language that creates the emotion that energizes others to high performance?

References

Agres, C., Edberg, D., & Igbaria, M. (1998). Transformation to virtual societies: Forces and issues. *Information Society*, 14(2), 71–82.

Avolio, B. J., Bass, B. M., & Jung, D. I. (1999). Re-examining the components of transformational and transactional leadership using the Multifactor Leadership Questionnaire. *Journal of Occupational and Organizational Psychology*, 72(4), 441–462.

Avolio, B. J., & Gibbons, T. C. (1988). Developing transformational leaders: A life span approach. In J. A. Congers & R. N. Kanungo (Eds.), *Charismatic leadership: The elusive factor in organizational effectiveness* (pp. 276–308). San Francisco: Jossey-Bass.

Bass, B. M. (1990). *Bass and Stogdill's handbook of leadership*. New York: Free Press.

Bass, B. M., & Avolio, B. J. (1994). *Improving organizational effectiveness through transformational leadership*. Thousand Oaks, CA: Sage.

Block, J. (1995). A contrarian view of the five factor approach to personality description. *Psychological Bulletin, 117*(2), 187–213.

Burns, J. M. (1978). *Leadership.* New York: Harper & Row.

Carlisle, C., & Phillips, D. A. (1984). The effects of enthusiasm training on selected teacher and student behaviors in preservice physical education teachers. *Journal of Teaching in Physical Education, 4*(1), 164–175.

Cassell, J., Huffaker, D., Tversky, D., & Ferriman, K. (2006). The language of online leadership: Gender and youth engagement on the Internet. *Developmental Psychology, 42*(3), 436–449.

Cattell, R. B. (1944). Interpretation of the twelve primary personality factors. *Journal of Personality, 13*(1), 55.

CNN Reports. (2007). *Workforce telecommuters.* Retrieved from www .cnn.com/2007/living/worklife/09/cb.work.home.advantage/index .html-72k-cached

Costa, P. T., & McCrae, R. R. (1988). Personality in adulthood: A six-year longitudinal study of self-reports and spouse ratings on the NEO Personality Inventory. *Journal of Personality and Social Psychology, 54*(5), 853–863.

Crandall, N. F., & Wallace, M. J. (1998). *Work and rewards in the virtual workplace: A "new deal" for organizations and employees.* New York: AMACOM.

Cree, V., & Macaulay, C. (2000). *Transfer of learning in professional and vocational education.* London: Routledge.

Dess, G., & Picken, J. (1999). *Beyond productivity: How leading companies achieve superior performance by leveraging their human capital.* New York: AMACOM.

Diemers, D. (1998). *The virtual triad: Society and man under the sign of virtuality.* Essay for the Ninth Honeywell Futurist Competition Europe, Munich.

Duarte, D. L., & Snyder, N. T. (2001). *Mastering virtual teams.* San Francisco: Jossey-Bass.

Dumdum, U. R., Lowe, K. B., & Avolio, B. J. (2002). A meta-analysis of transformational and transactional leadership correlates of effectiveness and satisfaction: An update and extension. In B. J. Avolio & F. J. Yammarino (Eds.), *Transformational and charismatic leadership: The road ahead* (pp. 36–66). Oxford, UK: Elsevier Science.

Eden, D., & Leviathan, U. (1975). Implicit leadership theory as a determinant of the factor structure underlying supervisory behavior. *Journal of Applied Psychology, 60*(6), 736–741.

Elenkov, D. S. (2002). Effects of leadership on organizational performance in Russian companies. *Journal of Business Research, 55*(6), 467–480.

Ehrhart, M. G., & Klein, K. J. (2001). Predicting followers' preferences for charismatic leadership: The influence of follower values and personality. *The Leadership Quarterly, 12*(2), 153–179.

Felfe, J., & Schyns, B. (2006). Personality and the perception of transformational leadership: The impact of extraversion, neuroticism, personal need for structure, and occupational self-efficacy. *Journal of Applied Social Psychology, 36*(3), 708–739.

Fisher, K., & Fisher, M. (2001). *The distance manager: A hands-on guide to managing off-site employees and virtual teams.* New York: McGraw-Hill.

Goldberg, L. R. (1990). An alternative "description of personality": The Big-Five factor structure. *Journal of Personality and Social Psychology, 59*(6), 1216–1229.

Gough, H. G. (1990) Testing for leadership with the California Psychological Inventory. In K. E. Clark & M. B. Clark (Eds.), *Measures of leadership* (pp. 355–379). West Orange, NJ: Leadership Library of America.

Howell, J. M., & Frost, P. J. (1989). A laboratory study of charismatic leadership. *Organizational Behavior and Human Decision Processes, 43*(2), 243–269.

Hoyt, C. L., & Blascovich, J. (2003). Transformational and transactional leadership in virtual and physical environments. *Small Group Research, 34*(6), 678–715.

IPIP. (n. d.). *International Personality Item Pool: A scientific collaboratory for the development of advanced measures of personality traits and other individual differences.* Available at http://ipip.ori.org/

John, O. P. (1990). The big-five factor taxonomy: Dimensions of personality in the natural language and in questionnaires. In L. A. Pervin (Ed.), *Handbook of personality theory and research* (pp. 66–100). New York: Guilford.

Judge, T. A., Piccolo, R., & Ilies, G. (2004). The forgotten ones? The validity of consideration and initiating structure in leadership research. *Journal of Applied Psychology, 89*(1), 36–51.

Jung, D. I., & Sosik, J. J. (2002). Transformational leadership in work groups: The role of empowerment, cohesiveness, and collective-efficacy on perceived group performance. *Small Group Research, 33*(3), 313–336.

Kark, R., & Shamir, B. (2002). The dual effect of transformational leadership: Priming relational and collective selves and further effects on followers. In B. J. Avolio & F. J. Yammarino (Eds.), *Transformational and charismatic leadership: The road ahead* (pp. 67–91). Oxford, UK: Elsevier Science.

Kark, R., Shamir, B., & Chen, G. (2003). The two faces of transformational leadership: Empowerment and dependency. *Journal of Applied Psychology, 88*, 246–255.

Keller, R. T. (1992). Transformational leadership and performance of research and development project groups. *Journal of Management, 18*(3), 489–501.

LeBrasseur, R., Whissell, R., & Ojha, A. (2002). Organisational learning, transformational leadership and implementation of continuous quality improvement in Canadian hospitals. *Australian Journal of Management, 27*(2), 141–162.

Lord, R. G., Brown, D. J., & Freiberg, S. J. (1999). Understanding the dynamics of leadership: The role of follower self-concepts in the leader/follower relationship. *Organizational Behavior and Human Decision Processes, 78*(3), 167–203.

Lord, G. L., De Vader, C. L., & Alliger, G. M. (1986). A meta-analysis of the relation between personality traits and leadership perceptions: An application of validity generalization procedures. *Journal of Applied Psychology, 71*(3), 402–410.

Lord, R. G., & Maher, K. J. (1991). *Leadership and information processing.* Boston: Routledge.

Mischel, W. (1977). The interaction of person and situation. In D. Magnusson & N. S. Endler (Eds.), *Personality at the crossroads: Current issues in interactional psychology* (pp. 333–352). Hillsdale, NJ: Erlbaum.

Pribram, K. (1969). The neurophysiology of remembering. *Scientific American, 220*(1), 73–89.

Pribram, K. (1977). *Languages in the brain.* Monterey, CA: Wadsworth.

Rai, S., & Sinha, A. K. (2000). Transformational leadership, organizational commitment, and facilitating climate. *Psychological Studies, 45*(1/2), 33–42.

Rowold, D. J., & Herrera, R. J. (2003). Inferring human phylogenies using forensic STR technology. *Forensic Science International, 133*(3), 260–266.

Salgado, J. F. (1997). The five factor model of personality and job performance in the European Community. *Journal of Applied Psychology, 82*(1), 30–43.

Salter, C., Carmody-Bubb, M., Duncan, P., & Green, M. T. (2007). Do transformational leaders speak differently? The impact of leaders' transformational communications in meeting follower's implicit leadership prototypes. In N. S. Huber & M. Harvey (Eds.), *Leadership: Impact, culture, and sustainability* (pp. 93–106). College Park, MD: International Leadership Association.

Schermerhorn, J. (2002). *Management.* Hoboken, NJ: Wiley.

Sosik, J. J., Avolio, B. J., Kahai, S. S., & Jung, D. I. (1998). Computer-supported work group potency and effectiveness: The role of transformational leadership, anonymity, and task interdependence. *Computers in Human Behavior, 14*(3), 491–511.

Southwell, B. G., Anghelcev, G., Himelboim, I., & Jones, J. (2007). Does user experience affect the relationship of control availability and control perception? *Computers in Human Behavior, 23*(1), 554–563.

Survey finds more employers offer telecommuting option. (2008, August 25). *San Antonio Business Journal.* Retrieved from http://sanantonio.bizjournals.com/sanantonio/stories/2008/8/25/daily26.html?t+printable

Tupes, E. C., & Christal, R. E. (1992). Recurrent personality factors based on trait ratings. *Journal of Personality, 60*(2), 225–245.

Winter, L., & Uleman, J. S. (1984). When are social judgments made? Evidence for the spontaneousness of trait inferences. *Journal of Personality and Social Psychology, 47*(2), 237–252.

Transforming Global Leadership

Applying the Lessons Learned from Brazil, India, and Nigeria toward the Development of an Integrated Model of Global Leadership

Karen J. Lokkesmoe

Global leadership is a hot topic in leadership and development circles today, but how is the term *global leadership* being defined and who formulates the definitions? Are those definitions evolving as the arenas expand in which global leadership is carried out and from which global leaders are emerging? How does one make the change from local to global leadership? And, what do we know about how one develops the capacities needed to make that transition? Much has been written about global leadership in the past decade. What are the lessons learned and what is missing? This chapter addresses a gap in the current literature in two key areas: perspectives and strategies focusing on developing countries and on public and nonprofit sectors. Further, it illustrates that to be inclusive of these sectors a more integrated global leadership framework is needed.

Defining the Topic and the Research Need

A review of the global leadership literature reveals a lack of input from noncorporate sectors or from developing countries in shaping the definitions and defining development strategies (Lokkesmoe, 2008, 2009), especially when these two sectors are combined. This research focuses on filling those gaps. Let us consider why it might matter that these perspectives are underrepresented. If so much has been published on global leadership, and some of it based on extensive research from around the world (House, Hanges, Javidan, Dorfman, & Gupta, 2004; Mendenhall, Osland, Bird, Oddou, & Maznevski, 2008; Osland, 2008), why is more research needed? In other words, what are the potential implications of the aforementioned gaps in the global leadership literature and knowledge? Here are a few that we might consider.

First, "global leadership is an emerging field" and the work to define the phenomenon of global leadership is far from complete (Osland, 2008, p. 62). A great deal of research and development continues to be done on many aspects of global leadership, including defining the construct, distinguishing behaviors and competencies, and identifying best practices in development and training. Including perspectives from arenas not yet well represented (that is, public and nonprofit sectors in developing counties) is an important element in that process.

Second, much of the research that has been done has been comparative research of how leadership is enacted around the world rather than research of *global leadership,* a construct that increasingly is being recognized as an entity unto itself and distinct from other forms of leadership (Adler, 2002; Lokkesmoe, 2008, 2009; Osland, 2008).

Third, corporate definitions and strategies (largely derived from Western, developed country perspectives) may be based on assumptions or conditions not shared in public/nonprofit or developing country environments, thereby calling into question the validity of their application in other contexts. If nothing else, strategies may be rejected from a perception that they are not applicable if a group feels underrepresented or excluded from the theory generation process.

Fourth, ignoring perspectives from the full range of stakeholders can greatly diminish the level of creativity and innovation that emerges or the level of acceptance of proposed strategies when addressing leadership (or other) challenges (Bryson, 1995; Hammer, 2007; Hammer & Bennett, 1998).

The Research Question

Based on this perceived gap in the literature and my interest in leadership development in and for people from developing countries, the research question as formulated for this study is as follows: What are effective global leadership development strategies for people from developing countries? Three secondary questions were developed as a means to explore this concept more fully.

1. What challenges do global leaders face when working internationally?
2. What competencies are essential to be an effective global leader?
3. What are the essential differences between global and local leadership?

Grounded theory research methods were used, with the intention of identifying the patterns that emerge from the data and potentially to develop a theoretical framework from which to continue to examine global leadership development in developing countries and in nonprofit environments. Briefly, preliminary surveys were utilized to gather biographical and baseline data relating to global leadership. Fourteen respondents with the highest level of international and leadership experience were selected to participate in personal interviews. Respondents represented public, private, and nonprofit sectors. They were almost evenly split between males and females, ranged in age from 32 to 62, had a minimum of one year of extensive global experience (most had much more), and worked in a range of industries including health care, journalism, government administration, finance, law, law enforcement, and international development.

A constant comparative method was used to analyze the data, pulling coding categories from the data itself and reviewing the interview texts and codes multiple times to identify emergent themes. These preliminary themes were then analyzed to develop a set of overarching themes. A full description of the methodology, findings, and data tables can be found in Lokkesmoe (2009).

Research Findings

Research findings fell into two distinct categories: those that were consistent across the group of respondents, and those that varied by country, sector, gender, age, or experience (the five biographical factors distinguished in this research). The first level of analysis looked at coded categories that were reported by 50 percent or more of the respondents. Data was later disaggregated by country, sector, gender, age, and experience. The findings are summarized here based on whether they were consistent across the group of respondents (reported by 50 percent or more) or were divergent (reported by 50 percent or more of a subgroup but not the full group). Summary data presenting the factors most frequently reported are available in Tables 13.1, 13.2, and

Table 13.1 Global Leadership Development Challenges Most Frequently Reported

Challenges	Frequency
Communication: language and meaning	11
Political or economic limitations	11
Being understood	9
Internal diversity	8
Resistance to change	8
Understanding local context	8
Transferability issues	7
Being willing to not have all the answers	5
Engaging around sensitive issues	5
Impact of power differences	5
Lack of cultural understanding	5

SOURCE: Data from interviews with respondents, n = 1 4.

Table 13.2 Global Leadership Competencies Most Frequently Reported

Competencies, Characteristics, and Behaviors	Frequency
Personal Competencies, Characteristics, and Behaviors	
Open-mindedness	13
Flexibility	12
Listening	10
Observe	10
Respect	9
Adaptability	8
Admit and learn from mistakes	8
Learn from others	8
Inclusiveness	7
Curiosity	7
Ethical	6
Humility	6
Equity and fairness	5
Honesty	5
Integrity	5
Patience	5
Selflessness	5
Tolerance	5
Intercultural Competencies, Characteristics, or Behaviors	
Understand other cultures	14
Broad perspective	13
Respect other cultures	12
Cognitive complexity	10
Cultural bridging	10
Cultural sensitivity	10
Global knowledge	10
Appreciate diversity	8

(Continued)

Table 13.2 *Continued*

Competencies, Characteristics, and Behaviors	Frequency
Interpersonal Competencies, Characteristics, or Behaviors	
Communication	13
Connecting with people	13
Building trust with others	10
Professional Competencies, Characteristics, or Behaviors	
Teamwork	11
Professional competence	10
Accountability	8
Empower/inspire others to act	6
Purpose: drive for results	5

SOURCE: Data from interviews with research participants, $n = 14$.

13.3. A full description of the methodology, findings, and data tables can be found in Lokkesmoe (2009). Responses focused on the four primary questions and were therefore analyzed by those categories (that is, *challenges, competencies, strategies,* and concepts of *global versus local leadership*).

Common Findings

There was a good deal of consistency across all the identifying factors, and by analyzing which concepts were reported by 50 percent or more of the full group a number of themes emerged. Because of the interconnectedness of the themes, a strict hierarchical order should not be assumed based on the order in which the themes are presented here, although I have attempted to report the most significant findings first.

Theme 1: Intercultural Competence Is a Critical Element of Global Leadership. Intercultural competencies play a promi-

Table 13.3 Global Leadership Development Strategies Most Frequently Reported

Strategies	Frequency
Gain International Experience	
Communicating with others	13
Exposure to difference	13
International exposure	13
Experiential learning	11
International exchanges	7
International education	6
Mentoring/role models/networking	5
Acquire Global Knowledge	
Sharing ideas with others	13
Education: formal	11
Media and technology	10
Professional training	10
Pay attention to details	9
Read and study	8
Know yourself/change yourself	6
Reflective practice	4
Address Contextual Factors through Policy Advocacy	
Education policy change	6
Don't make assumptions about transferability	5
Learn how to use media effectively	5
Support democratic processes	5
Focus on future/youth	4
Focus positive examples and success stories	4
Understanding the power dynamics	4

SOURCE: Data from interviews with research participants, $n = 14$.

nent role in the responses to all four of the research questions. The eight intercultural competencies were those reported most consistently by the full group of respondents, with all eight reported by 50 percent or more of the respondents. In total, 21 of the 24 competencies reported by 50 percent or more are related either directly or indirectly to intercultural competencies (that is, listed by interculturalists as key to intercultural competence). Examples of such competencies are open-mindedness, flexibility, understanding, and adaptability). Additionally, intercultural competencies and intercultural challenges were typically those factors described as having the greatest impact on success as one moved from a local to a global leadership context. More than 50 percent of the challenges reported described negotiating intercultural interactions. These ranged from basic language skills to a more profound understanding of the values and belief systems present in the context. Two of the three categories of recommended strategies also have an intercultural focus: *gaining intercultural experience* and *acquiring global knowledge*. These include strategies such as formal education and training as well as informal interactions through internships, volunteerism, social interactions, independent explorations of topics of interest (for example, art, literature, history, geography, anthropology, and music), and travel.

The need for developing a broad perspective or a global mind-set (an attitude of openness and flexibility, inclusive of multiple cultural perspectives) was articulated in a variety of ways. This factor was present in the lists of competencies that were reported, in the strategies recommended, in the challenges encountered, as well as identified as one of the factors, when lacking, that impedes effective global leadership. In summary, the role of intercultural competence in effective global leadership was the most prominent theme that emerged from the data and was present in nearly all aspects of the findings.

Theme 2: Global Leaders Need to Pay Attention to the Local Context. There are several facets of this theme that relate to individual as well as societal demands. Closely linked to intercultural understanding and the need for developing a broad perspective is the need to successfully negotiate the local context, including the political, economic, and societal contextual factors. This means much more than just analyzing the local market; it refers to developing an understanding of the multiple aspects of the local environment and being able to connect to people in ways that will enable leaders to understand the local issues and to propose strategies that are acceptable and likely to garner followership. Along with understanding the cultural aspects of a society, leaders must recognize aspects of the local contexts such as political, religious, and economic factors—especially in Nigeria.

These leadership challenges are similar to those expressed by people working in public and nonprofit sectors around the world. Because constituent groups are not limited to those with an interest in a specific product or service, but frequently include the society as a whole, the need to be able to relate to the full set of stakeholders is key to success (Bryson, 1995). The stakeholder groups tend to be related in a less hierarchical manner with no single person or entity in charge. Power is shared (Bryson & Crosby, 1992; Crosby & Bryson, 2005) and requires more collaborative, participatory leadership (Lipman-Blumen, 2000). Overall, a need for a more inclusive context for global leadership was expressed.

Also included in this category is the need for understanding contexts in which democratic processes are less well developed and less well enforced than in many developed countries. This includes issues of transparency, accountability, rule of law, corruption, nepotism, and cultural practices (including authority granted by age, seniority, gender, or family status). Although not all groupings reported this at the same intensity, there is a shared belief that less stable, more chaotic systems operate in developing countries and affect how individuals carry out leadership tasks.

Theme 3: Global Leadership Varies in Scope and Magnitude from Local Leadership. Although there are differences in how respondents view global leadership, there are some commonalities as well. Operating within an understanding that global leadership refers to leading a team, project, company, or country in a global (diverse) context, challenges faced and competencies required for success were identified by 50 percent or more of the respondents (see Tables 13.1 and 13.2). There was a consensus that global leadership differs from local leadership in both scope and magnitude. A global leader not only needs a broader set of competencies than a local leader but is also called upon to conduct his or her work in an environment that is significantly more diverse, more intense, and continually changing, thus requiring more and more finely tuned leadership competencies than in a local context. As stated earlier, intercultural competencies form the core of what is seen as facilitating the transformation from local to global effectiveness.

Theme 4: There Are Both Challenges and Rewards to Global Leadership. Respondents readily identified both challenges and rewards of global leadership. Challenges included communication issues and physical and emotional challenges related to the isolation and separation from family and a home support environment when working in another country. This was especially true for those who worked in areas where access to technology and communications systems were not readily available. Communication issues included language differences (verbal and nonverbal) and understanding the implicit meaning and the underlying values of others. All reported the experience as having provided great value to them personally and professionally. Most used statements such as, "It was enriching," "It really enriches your life," "It makes you a richer person." The idea of having gained a "broader understanding of the world" was also prominent. Despite some cases of great personal challenges, none of the participants expressed regret for having had global assignments or the desire to discontinue working in such arenas. This concept is consistent with previous findings and needs little elaboration, but one aspect that is interesting, and that I come back to later, is that among the benefits of working at the global level articulated by participants were greater transparency, accountability, and more reliable systems for advancement and rewards.

Theme 5: Global Leadership Development Strategies Are Diverse and Multileveled. There are many means to acquire the knowledge and skills needed by global leaders as is evident in a list of forty-four strategies (see Lokkesmoe, 2009) reported by the respondents. There are three categories of strategies: *gaining international experience, acquiring global knowledge*, and *addressing contextual factors through policy advocacy*. Only 11 of the 44 were reported by 50 percent or more of the respondents. Strategies could be pursued through either formal or informal means of learning or at an individual level or an organizational level, perhaps indicating a distinction between leader development and leadership development similar to that outlined by the Center for Creative Leadership (McCauley & Van Velsor, 2004). None of the items in the final category, addressing contextual factors through policy advocacy, were reported by 50 percent or more of the full group of respondents but were reported at significant levels by the respondents from Nigeria.

The respondents demonstrated that many kinds of strategies and multilevel strategies are important. They stressed both formal and informal ways of enhancing one's global leadership competencies and reported that experience plays a key role in the process, that a multidisciplinary approach is desirable, and that the process is developmental and takes time.

Divergent Findings

In addition to the many common themes articulated by the respondents, there were also some areas of divergence that present interesting contrasts. In some cases the themes varied by country, sector, gender, age, or experience. Due to space limitations, only the most significant of those differences are reported here.

Comparisons between Global and Local Leadership. Although the general consensus was that global leadership presents greater challenges and requires greater skills than local leadership, there were two respondents (from different countries and different sectors) who felt that local leadership is more demanding than global leadership. They felt that due to the greater levels of accountability, transparency, and reliability of the global work environment that global leadership presents fewer challenges. Both stated that the high level of diversity within their countries and less than reliable governance systems were contributing factors. This is a minority opinion and was refuted by other respondents from their countries; however, it poses an interesting topic for further research. If experience in this kind of an environment aids in developing the capacity to deal with diversity, then, would people from these environments have an advantage in global leadership positions?

The Role of Contextual Factors in Global Leadership. In general there was a consistent view that a more integrated and comprehensive global leadership framework is required that includes a broader array of contextual factors, but the relative role of these factors varied slightly. The importance of ethical and political factors and policy-level development strategies was most prominent in Nigeria and more prominent in Brazil than in India. There was greater stress on ethical and political factors related to integrity, honesty, ethics, and humility. The role of personal factors and self-determination was more prominent among the private sector (and slightly more in India). Indian respondents also more frequently reported items of an introspective nature, such as reflective practice, patience, and knowing oneself. Respondents from Brazil and Nigeria placed a greater emphasis on youth-focused and educational strategies and on promoting positive public role models through acknowledging and rewarding examples of ethical (and effective) leadership. They also stressed collaborative, team, and organizational leadership more in Brazil and Nigeria. Respondents from Nigeria attributed their understanding of leadership to their religious faith fairly consistently. Male respondents and those from the private sector more frequently reported on the intensity of the challenges of global work, while female respondents reported greater frustration with status quo and inequitable treatment. Female respondents listed fewer challenges and higher numbers of strategies overall.

The Role of Technology in Global Leadership. Although there were no questions directly asking about technology, several of the respondents mentioned it specifically and identified technology as an important factor in how global leadership is carried out.

It will come as no surprise that the findings reinforce the notion that the factors in each individual leadership context are considered important to that context. Although it is clear that not all factors are equally important in all cases, leaders need to consider the full range of factors to determine which ones require attention in each case.

The Integrated Model of Global Leadership Development

Based on this research, my own experience in the field, and a synthesis of existing models, I have articulated an integrated model of global leadership development. This model consists of four competency domains that global leaders must draw upon, as well as an array of contextual factors that influence the conceptualizations and enactment of effective global leadership practices (see Figure 13.1).

Figure 13.1 Integrated Global Leadership Development Model

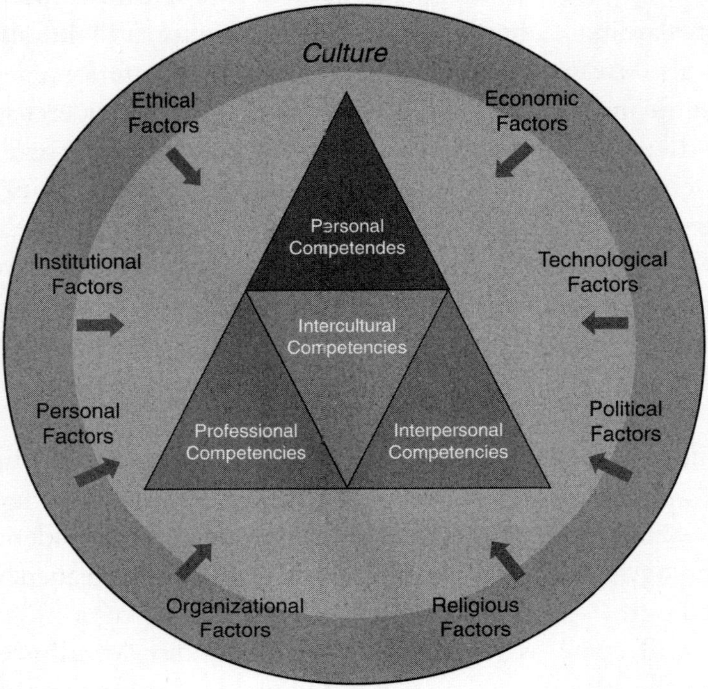

Four Domains of Leadership Competencies

The four domains of leadership competencies that a global leader needs are *personal*, *interpersonal*, *professional*, and *intercultural competencies*. My definitions for each domain vary only slightly from those that emerged from the data in this study and from existing models (Brake, 1997; Osland & Taylor, 2003; Rosen, 2000).

1. *Personal competencies.* This domain includes capabilities that one develops as an individual and personal characteristics. Capabilities include listening, observing, and basic language and communication skills such as writing and learning a foreign language. Characteristics include open-mindedness, flexibility, honesty, and integrity.

2. *Interpersonal competencies*. This domain includes capabilities that facilitate a leader's interactions or relationships with others, such as interpersonal communication, empathy, emotional intelligence, and networking.

3. *Professional competencies*. This domain includes knowledge bases pertaining specifically to the craft of a particular vocation (for example, medicine, education, finance, engineering, law), and more general competencies needed by professionals (for example, organizational expertise, visioning, teamwork, and empowering others).

4. *Intercultural competencies*. This domain requires capabilities such as understanding other cultures, cultural bridging, cognitive complexity, and coping with ambiguity. It is clear from the research that intercultural competence is not simply one factor but consists of a set of competencies that are important in their own right and that influence other competencies. For this reason, I have included intercultural competencies in the center of the model, rather than subsumed under or distributed among the other sets of competencies. As the model illustrates, intercultural competencies interact with and influence the other competencies. A global leader must constantly be seeking a global perspective by revisiting his/her personal, interpersonal, and professional competencies through the lens of intercultural competencies. We see ourselves, our interactions with others, and our professional roles and responsibilities differently through an intercultural lens than through our own cultural lens. It is this central role of intercultural competencies that indicates that these competencies lie at the heart of transforming local leaders into global leaders.

Interconnectedness. The interconnectedness of the four competencies within the larger triangle shown in Figure 13.1 illustrates how they influence one another. How adept we become at intercultural communication is highly influenced by our basic command of the language and how well we communicate with others. If one does not have solid professional capabilities, leadership locally or globally will be difficult. Although I have identified intercultural competencies as a central influencing factor, it is clear that the specific relationship among these four competencies requires further research.

Global leadership, as seen in the model, takes place within a specific context that is influenced by many factors. These factors, in turn, either affect the cultural context or are affected by the cultural context. For this reason, they are illustrated as part of the global leadership context within the broader cultural context.

Conclusion

This new theoretical model has yet to be fully tested. A few groups of international leaders have reviewed the model and it was well received, but much more work remains to be done. As with most grounded theory research, more questions arise than are answered. Some potential questions for future research include: Will the model hold true in a larger sample, with more countries? How can the skill sets within each global competency be further refined? Does coming from an environment that is highly fluid and highly diverse present any advantages or disadvantages for a leader at the global level? Could an integrated model of global leadership development offer a greater opportunity for transformation within a developing country context? How does an organization or country address policy-level strategies for enhancing global leadership capacity without effective global leaders? What is the role of technology in how emerging leaders acquire and enhance their global knowledge and global capacities? How does one balance the need for core capacities in a specific field with the need to gain experience with diversity and multidisciplinarity?

Much work is being done in this area and much remains to be done. My hope is that this research has illuminated the path for greater numbers and more effective global leaders from developing countries and within public and nonprofit sectors.

References

Adler, N. J. (2002). *International dimensions of organizational behavior* (4th ed.). Cincinnati, OH: South-Western.

Brake, T. (1997). *The global leader: Critical factors for creating the world class organization.* Chicago: Irwin Professional.

Bryson, J. M. (1995). *Strategic planning for public and nonprofit organization: A guide to strengthening and sustaining organizational achievement* (rev. ed.). San Francisco: Jossey-Bass.

Bryson, J. M., & Crosby, B. C. (1992). *Leadership for the common good: Tackling public problems in a shared-power world.* San Francisco: Jossey-Bass.

Crosby, B. C., & Bryson, J. M. (2005). *Leadership for the common good: Tackling public problems in a shared-power world* (2nd ed.). San Francisco: Jossey-Bass.

Hammer, M. R. (2007). *Intercultural Development Inventory Manual* (v. 3). Ocean Pines, MD: IDI, LLC.

Hammer, M. R. (2009). The Intercultural Development Inventory (IDI): An approach for assessing and building intercultural competence. In M. A. Moodian (Ed.), *Contemporary leadership and intercultural competence: Understanding and utilizing cultural diversity to build successful organizations* (pp. 203–218).Thousand Oaks, CA: Sage.

Hammer, M. R., & Bennett, M. J. (1998). The Intercultural Development Inventory (IDI) Manual. Self published.

House R. J., Hanges, P. J., Javidan, M., Dorfman, P. W., & Gupta, V. (2004). *Culture, leadership, and organizations: The GLOBE study of 62 societies.* Thousand Oaks, CA: Sage.

Lipman-Blumen, J. (2000). *Connective leadership: Managing in a changing world.* Oxford, UK; New York: Oxford University Press.

Lokkesmoe, K. J. (2008). Discovering the power of the Intercultural Development Inventory as a global leadership development tool. In M. Harvey & J. D. Barbour (Eds.), *Building Leadership Bridges 2008* (pp. 65–81). College Park, MD: International Leadership Association.

Lokkesmoe, K. J. (2009). *A grounded theory study of effective global leadership development strategies: Perspectives from Brazil, India, and Nigeria.* Doctoral thesis, University of Minnesota, 2009.

McCauley, C. D., & Van Velsor, E. (Eds.). (2004). *The Center for Creative Leadership handbook of leadership development* (2nd ed.). San Francisco: Jossey-Bass.

Mendenhall, M., Osland, J., Bird, A., Oddou, G., & Maznevski, M. (Eds.). (2008). *Global leadership: Research, practice and development.* New York: Routledge.

Osland, J. (2008). An overview of the global leadership literature. In M. Mendenhall, J. Osland, A. Bird, G. Oddou, & M. Maznevski (Eds.), *Global leadership: Research, practice and development* (pp. 34–63). New York: Routledge.

Osland, J. S., & Taylor, S. (2003). *Course packet: Developing global leaders.* Summer Institute for Intercultural Communication. Unpublished manuscript.

Rosen, R. T. (2000). *Global literacies: Lessons on business leadership and national cultures: A landmark study of CEOs from 28 countries.* New York: Simon & Schuster.

Exploring Leadership
for Transformation

Tom Beech, Juana Bordas, Prasad Kaipa,
and Eliane Ubalijoro

This chapter is taken from portions of the International Leadership Association (ILA) Annual Global Conference Opening Keynote Session, "Exploring Leadership for Transformation," on November 12, 2009, in Prague, Czech Republic. A transcript of the complete panel session is available from the International Leadership Association. The session's goal was to explore leadership for transformation from a range of perspectives, raise questions, stimulate conference participants' imaginations, and start conversations that would spill over into the rest of the conference and beyond.

The session began with several inspirational video clips from prominent world leaders, activists, and scholars. Afterward, panel members offered their insights and perspectives. This chapter presents selected comments from the moderator and panel members that highlight perspectives from each person's rich and diverse background, culture, and philosophy.

Panelists included Juana Bordas, president of Mestiza Leadership International in Denver, Colorado; Prasad Kaipa, founder and executive director of the Center for Leadership, Innovation and Change at the Indian School of Business; and Eliane Ubalijoro, professor at McGill University's Institute for the Study of International Development. Moderator for the session was Tom Beech, president and CEO of the Fetzer Institute in Kalamazoo, Michigan.

Video Introductions

Moderator Tom Beech introduced five video segments featuring Archbishop Emeritus Desmond Tutu in two segments; Nobel Prize winner Rigoberta Menchu Tum; author and teacher Parker Palmer; and leading scholar Karen Armstrong.

Tom Beech, Moderator

The first video allows us to hear from one of our world's great leaders, Archbishop Emeritus Desmond Tutu. This segment comes from a public conversation he and I had in the presence of a large audience in Kalamazoo in 2008. We will hear him talk about the importance of encouraging leadership in young people and avoiding our tendency as adults to smother youthful idealism.

The next video segment is from Rigoberta Menchu Tum, who was awarded the Nobel Peace Prize in 1992 for her work on behalf of social justice and the rights of indigenous peoples. She has been a courageous defender of her native Mayan culture. It is important to know that her entire family—her mother, her father, and her brothers—were tortured and killed by the Guatemalan army. Despite this, in this video she speaks about the importance of living in harmony and peace, within oneself and with others.

The third video segment returns to another statement from the same conversation that Archbishop Tutu and I had a couple of summers ago. He recalls a visit to Darfur and reflects on the amazing resilience of the refugees and also on the notion that leadership is rooted in service and in selflessness and in human goodness. The fourth video segment is a short statement from author and teacher, Parker Palmer. Parker has done pioneering work on the importance of inner strength, awareness, and integrity, what he calls "the wisdom of the heart," as the well from which true leadership comes. He is the founder of the Center for Courage and Renewal.

This last segment focuses on the importance of compassion as a transformative force in our world. Karen Armstrong, leading scholar on world religions, won a Technology, Entertainment, Design (TED) Prize last year and her wish was to launch a Global Charter for Compassion. In bringing the topic of compassion into our dialogue, we are not necessarily talking about religion. We invite you to come at this from your own philosophical perspective. But we are suggesting that compassion—the act of putting ourselves in another's shoes, accepting others who are different from us, treating others as we would want to be treated—is an important aspect of leadership.

Perspectives from Videos: World Leaders, Activists, and Scholars

Desmond Tutu: Youthful Idealism

May I start off first by paying a tribute to young people; they have this incredible idealism. They really do believe the world can become a better place, until they are affected by us oldies, with our cynicisms. And one wants to say, look here, don't let us muck you up. Go on dreaming that, yes, poverty can become history; we can in fact live in a world without war. Far too frequently the kind of coverage we get in the media is only about kids going astray. And I say, are we aware of the pressures under which our children live today? What should surprise us is not that some kids may go astray. What should be surprising us and making us celebrate is the fact that so many of them don't.

Rigoberta Menchu Tum: Indigenous People

The Creator for me is the Heart of the Sky, the Heart of the Earth. The Creator is life. We are in transit through this time. I'm a part of the Indigenous Peoples. I come from these cultures that date back thousands of years. And for those age-old cultures, Nature is their only mother, where you always have to live.

I am Mayan, and my time is Mayan. My logic is Mayan. And my relationship with the dead is a very harmonious relationship. It is not a relationship of fighting, of confrontation. My relationship with my loved ones who have died is a relationship of dialogue, of interchange, of asking for much positive strength, and not negative strength. So I live in peace with my loved ones who have died. I live at peace with my life, and also wish to live in peace with others.

Desmond Tutu: Darfur

We went to Darfur. Now all the descriptions that you might have heard of that place are nowhere near telling you about the reality. It is awful. But I took away two particular impressions. We went to this displaced persons camp and saw the shacks where they live. The shelters are just flimsy, flimsy things that keep out neither the sun, nor the heat, nor the cold. We had a meeting with about two hundred of the displaced persons, and at some point somebody said something, and they laughed and laughed. You look around and you say, how could they possibly still have the capacity to laugh? The one thing I took away from that experience is that the resilience of the human spirit is amazing. And then, the other thing that struck us so powerfully was the dedication, the commitment of the humanitarian workers. Almost all of them were people who came from countries where they lead a very comfortable life. But here they were, in Darfur, and some of them had been coming repeatedly. We went away, devastated by the condition of the people but also exhilarated by this example of what human beings are. You and I are actually creatures who are created for goodness.

Parker Palmer: Wisdom of the Heart

The wisdom of the heart always tells us, you are worthy, you are precious, you are of profound value as you stand, as a human being. And when you take that vulnerability to the voice of power, which wants to hold you down, which wants to oppress you, which wants to manipulate you, something happens that doesn't happen overnight. You need to keep working at it, you need to keep practicing that vulnerability, you need to keep invoking the powers of the heart. But I don't know any significant social change that has not required and been animated by that kind of movement of the heart, to both claim my own integrity and to witness to it, in the face of power. It often means sacrifice, great sacrifice. People have lost their lives for doing this. But ultimately the heart is the place in which we learn what's worth living for, and therefore what's worth dying for. I don't mean to overly dramatize that. I'm not talking about everyone going to some kind of martyrdom. I'm simply talking about growing our own capacity to express our deepest humanity in places where it would seem unwelcome, in places where the reception may be hostile, and to trust that in the end, what's going to count as we're taking our last breath is our own answer to the question, was I fully present in the world with my own truth, with my own identity and integrity, as much as humanly possible, as much as I was able, as much as I knew how?

Karen Armstrong: Compassion

Compassion is part of our humanity. But like all human characteristics, compassion needs to be cultivated. We have to work on it just as a dancer uses her natural powers of movement to create almost unearthly beauty. So, too, we need to cultivate compassion, and if we do this, as Confucius said, "all day and every day," looking into our own hearts, discovering what it is that gives us pain and then refusing under any circumstance whatsoever to inflict that pain on anybody else, all day and every day, then we begin to cultivate new capacities of mind and heart. It takes us beyond the prism of selfishness and self-interest that holds us back from our best selves.

Perspectives from Panelists

Moderator Beech asked panel members to reflect on several issues raised in the video clips: the importance of leadership among young people; the need for sharing and openness in leadership development; and the power of resiliency. In the section to follow, comments from panelists are taken from the discussion, and highlights from those comments are collated beneath each panelist's name.

Juana Bordas: Intergenerational Power, Connectedness, and Resilience

Like Desmond Tutu said, young people believe we can have world peace; we can clean up our planet; we can eliminate poverty. So I think when we talk about young people it's no longer true that the older generation has something that they don't have. The exciting question is how do we build this circle of leadership, this intergenerational power that comes from tapping into their idealism so that a shared vision and sense of possibility stays alive? . . .

I want to follow up on Rigoberta Menchu Tum's comment concerning her Mayan philosophy. The Mayans believed that we were mirrors for each other and that you could only know yourself through the eyes of another. In their tradition, when they would greet each other they would say, *En La kech*, "I am another yourself" or "I am in you and you are in me." This acknowledges that you and I are connected and, furthermore, only by you looking at me and letting me know what you see do I become and understand who I am. . . .

I think all of us are here only because of the resiliency of others—the sacrifices and contributions of our mothers and fathers. I'm an immigrant and I am here because of the resiliency and dedication of my parents. My mother was willing to scrub floors and serve food so that I could be here with you today, so I could get an education. I grew up in the segregated south. I witnessed the resiliency of African Americans who, through centuries of oppression, had a saying, "If it doesn't kill you, it will make you stronger."

We have only progressed as a people because of the resiliency of our ancestors, of our parents, of those who came before us. They taught us that when you have a setback, just as we talked about challenges or learning opportunities, when you fall or stumble it's going to make you stronger. But you have to learn from your challenges and mistakes. You have to continue and not give up.

This is where the inner resiliency comes, and I think externally that brings a certain reliability and trust that other people will have in you. Regardless of what kinds of obstacles we have, we're going to face them together. As we come out of these we are going to be better and stronger and more ourselves for having overcome these challenges.

Eliane Ubalijoro: Unity, Vulnerability, and Perseverance

Listening to this clip [from Bishop Tutu] took me to a special place, a hard place, about the importance of us listening to young people and looking to them also for solutions. After the 1994 genocide in Rwanda where I am from, it took a long time for the country to rebuild itself, and during that phase there were episodes of insurgence. The Interahamwe, who had killed a lot of people during the genocide, were trying to come back and create fear in the country. In a particular school where they had come, they asked these children who were in the boarding school to separate, on one side the Hutus, and the other side the Tutsis, so that they could kill the Tutsis. And in this school there was a girl whose father had been a killer and he had been imprisoned. She refused to give away her Tutsi friends and because of that she died and a number of children died that night. But some did survive and were able to tell the story, and every year now in Rwanda we have a national heroes day and on that day we remember the example of the youth, these teenagers, who inspired us to say, as Parker Palmer was saying, sometimes we have to be able to sacrifice even our lives. It's not that they wanted to do this but their belief in the unity that we have was greater than their fear of death. . . .

When I think of power, our power for me lies in our greatest vulnerabilities. Are we willing to look at those places where we know we're not that great and are we willing to work with others so that they can pull us out of those spaces? There's a quote by Maureen Murdock that I'd like to share with all of you: "Our strength is not in the things that represent what is familiar, comfortable, or positive but in our fear and even in our resistance to change. These areas of discomfort grow us but these areas cannot be moved forward without the help of others and it starts by bringing forward humility" [1990]. Can I admit my spaces of fear, my spaces of incompetence? Can I let Juana, Prasad, and Tom share with me, help me move forward? Can I help each of you? Can you help me in the spaces where I know I need strength, and do I have that humility to go forward to you and say will you be my friend and will you help me move forward? . . .

One image that comes to mind is that women in the refugee camps in Darfur originally had to go out of the camps to get water and every time they left the camps they risked being raped. But it was the only way for them to get water for their children so every day, knowing the risks that were in front of them, they would still go out there to get water. When I think of these women and any problem comes to me, I can't back down, because I don't have to face what they had to face. The struggles faced by women in Darfur with new UN guidelines hopefully will not be faced by others, as having water close or within the refugee camps has become a priority in the design and planning of refugee camps [UNHCR, 2006]. So this is something that's changed to help these women, realizing that spirit of perseverance, saying, "I am going to go on so my child can have water." If the women of Darfur were given more opportunities, we have no idea how amazingly they could contribute to this world. Knowing that space, for me, gives me the drive every day to say no matter what, I will move forward. I may fail, I may stumble, I may be humiliated today but I have to try.

Prasad Kaipa: Appreciation, Alignment, and Inner Transformation

While I was looking at the clips, several things came to my mind. If we want to bring about a transformation in the next generation, we have to role-model it and look for changes that other people are bringing in their lives with appreciation, ourselves. Archbishop Tutu and others teach us of the importance of appreciating the perspective of others. What you appreciate, appreciates. It's very easy to forget to appreciate—especially when we are working with our children, working with younger generations. We are quick to point out what doesn't work, what is wrong with them, what they need to change, but not what we appreciate in them. Appreciation opens the heart to deeper listening, and only through the heart can we actually bring about a lasting, sustainable transformation. . . .

If we map management to Indian Kundalini Energy model, the heart level is the first level in which leadership appears. Leadership does not emerge until the heart is open, and that connects with the wisdom of the heart that Parker Palmer talked about. The first three chakras are about various management approaches. So these three chakras represent—roughly and metaphorically—management by fear, management by incentive, management by power and control. Resilience and resilient leadership begins at the heart chakra or fourth chakra. The fifth chakra or throat chakra is about finding your voice and communicating your own story in a way that brings other people forward to ignite their own genius. If you don't become arrogant at this level and recognize that it is not about you as a leader creating followers—it's about developing more leaders and there are many remarkable people like you in the world—then jealousy subsides and you create a leadership field with diverse leaders operating at their best and bringing about transformation in their own way. That is what the sixth chakra represents. And then the seventh chakra is about recognizing that everybody around you is a child of God. There is nothing missing even though they may be operating at their own level and every one of us are leaders.

So what the Kundalini metaphor taught me is that leadership for transformation is closely connected with appreciation, love, clarity about our own story, and with creating opportunities for people to tap into their own inner genius. That doesn't mean the challenge doesn't go away, though. I would say once we are grounded in ourselves and are nurturing the love or affection or caring and compassion for each other we can then take on a challenge and succeed. If other people present us with a challenge, we can choose to stretch and use it as an opportunity to grow beyond. So there is a place for challenge in our lives, and how we frame it and how we look at it will make us more resilient.

Tom Beech, Moderator

Just a few weeks ago a number of us from the Fetzer Institute were in Vancouver and had the great privilege of listening to the Dalai Lama over a period of days, and I was struck by the number of times when someone would ask him a question, he would think for a minute and then he'd say, "I don't know." This is a person who you expect will always have an answer, but he honestly would say, sometimes with humor and with great humility, "I just don't know." How important is that kind of sharing and that kind of openness in leadership development? . . .

We've offered a variety of ideas about leadership for your consideration, and amidst this variety one thing is very clear to me, and that is that our world is crying for leadership: leadership from people in formal positions of power and authority, leadership from the grassroots, leadership in every field of endeavor. This is leadership that must come from deep within us and must exist deeply among us. It's the leadership that brings hope in the face of cruelty, resilience in response to disillusionment and humility and humor when authority gets full of itself. It's leadership that faces fear with compassion, love, and forgiveness.

References and Further Readings

Armstrong, K. (2009). *The case for God.* New York: Knopf.

Bordas, J. (2007). *Salsa, soul, and spirit: Leadership for a multicultural age.* San Francisco: Berrett-Koehler.

Gervais, M., Ubalijoro, E., & Nyirabega, E. (2009). *Girlhood in a post-conflict situation: The case of Rwanda. Agenda,* No 79, 13–23. http://www.agenda.org.za

Kaipa, P. (2005). *Discontinuous learning: Igniting the genius within by aligning self, work and family.* Retrieved from http://kaipagroup.com/books/discontinuous_learning.html

Kaipa, P. (2005). *Six principles for 21st century leaders.* Retrieved from http://kaipagroup.com/articles/six_principles/six_principles_pg1.php

Murdock, M. (1990). *The heroine's journey.* Boston: Shambhala.

Palmer, P. J. (2004). *A hidden wholeness: The journey toward an undivided life: Welcoming the soul and weaving community in a wounded world.* San Francisco: Jossey-Bass.

Tutu, D., & Abrams, D. C. (2004). *God has a dream: A vision of hope for our time.* New York: Doubleday.

Ubalijoro, E. (2008). *Seizing the moment to co-create a bright future.* Kigali, Rwanda: Imbuto Foundation.

UNHCR. (2006). *Access to water in refugee situations: Survival, health and dignity for refugees.* Retrieved from www.un.org/waterforlifedecade/pdf/unhcr_water_brochure.pdf

The Friendship of Tung-Shan and Yün-Yen

Mark Nepo

After a long apprenticeship and friendship with his master, Tung-Shan (807–869) asked Yün-Yen, "After you have died, what should I say if someone wants to know what you were like?" After a long silence, Yün-Yen quietly replied, "Say Just this person." Tung-Shan seemed puzzled and his friend put his arm around him and continued, "You must be very careful, since you are carrying this Great Matter." They spoke no more about it. Later when Yün-Yen died, Tung-Shan wandered in a stream in his grief, only to see his own reflection; carried for the moment by everyone's reflection. It was then that he understood what his friend meant. Later still, having crossed the stream and his grief, Tung-Shan wrote, "If you look for the truth outside yourself, it gets farther and farther away."

Name Index

Subject Index

Page references followed by *fig* indicate an illustrated figure; followed by *t* indicate a table.